LOOKING AT BUILDINGS
THE EAST RIDING

Hazel Moffat ● David Neave

LOOKING AT BUILDINGS

CONTENTS

Eddie Ryle-Hodges

Eddie Ryle-Hodges

BM Photographic Services

TOP RIGHT: Kirkham Priory gatehouse.
CENTRE RIGHT: Wallingfen Methodist Church.
BOTTOM RIGHT: Punch Hotel, Hull.

ABOUT THIS BOOK

Buildings shape our perception of the past and reflect the priorities of the present.

This book focuses on some of the most distinctive and rewarding buildings in the towns and countryside of the East Riding. The following pages explore in what ways they contribute to the character of the region. What makes them typical of their period? And how are they being treated today?

Modest village housing provides an insight into local building materials and practice, while the great stone churches include some of the most magnificent medieval creations anywhere in England. The Georgian period saw the development of the elegant market town of Beverley, based on agricultural prosperity to which the grand farmsteads and the wind and water mills of the countryside still bear witness. Country mansions with parks and estate villages, created through the all-important patronage of rural landowners, contrast with seaside resorts promoted by optimistic developers, while the port of Hull offers a fascinating mixture of merchants' and workers' housing, functional dock buildings, and Victorian and Edwardian civic grandeur. Finally, the late twentieth century offers some radically different approaches: bold new architectural forms beside traditional reconstruction; sensitive repair and adaptation along with less tactful alteration.

Each illustrated double page discusses a different theme, and includes

■ Background information on the historical and architectural context

■ 'Questions to consider', including ideas for discussion and further investigation

■ Details of places to visit

At the back of the book are

■ An illustrated glossary of architectural terms and a time chart of architectural styles

■ Details on source material and further reading

In this book there is room only to introduce a selection of the buildings and topics. Many more are covered in the more comprehensive survey, *The Buildings of England: Yorkshire: York and the East Riding*, by Nikolaus Pevsner and David Neave, Penguin Books, 1995, which can be used as a companion to *Looking at Buildings*. Like every volume in the *Buildings of England* series, this includes both a general introduction to the architecture of the region and descriptions of all important places and buildings, arranged alphabetically.

W: West
N: North etc.

Norman detail – see glossary drawings, p.33

Perp: Perpendicular
Dec: Decorated
For Gothic styles, see pp.8–9 and drawings on p.33

Nonconformist chapels – see p.19

Farmhouse and cottage design – see pp.14–15, p.20

Rural industry – see p.21

C13: Thirteenth century
C14: Fourteenth century, etc.

Church Monuments – see pp.10–11

684   SKELTON · SKIDBY

of Doncaster. Tripartite segmental-arched window to centre on second floor with pediment above. A few later C18 features survive inside including the staircase and some panelling.

Gothic mid-C19 LODGE, grey brick and slate with stone details.

SKERNE

0050

ST LEONARD. A small church consisting of rendered nave, chancel and porch, and an ashlar (W) tower. After the drabness of the exterior the interior is a great surprise. There are substantial Norman parts, namely the chancel arch of three orders of shafts with zigzag, the W wall with a blank arch, the S doorway, of which a few pieces of beakhead remain, a S window blocked and partly revealed, and a chancel N window. So nave and chancel are both Norman. A N aisle was built in the C13 and although demolished the blocked arcade remains, visible inside. The piers are quatrefoil, except for one with extra shafts in the diagonals. The E respond has a fillet. The arches are double-chamfered. Also (C13) the low-side lancet in the chancel. The E window is three-light (Dec) with big mouchettes. (Perp) W tower. The church was 're-stored' in the 1840s. – (MONUMENTS.) They will give you a fright. They are displayed upright and face you as you enter, and they are grotesquely retooled. Male figure in civilian clothes with crossed legs and sword c.1340. A semi-effigy of a woman in a quatrefoil with her feet visible in half a quatrefoil below, also mid-C14. Between them is a small figure of what appears to be an infant in swaddling clothes. Could this chrysom figure also be C14?

Attractive former SCHOOL and MASTER'S HOUSE of 1877 by *J. H. Carroll* of Scarborough. Slate roof with decorative ridge-tiles and a pretty bell-turret. Opposite is a single-storey C18 whitewashed brick and pantile cottage with an adjoining former (WESLEYAN CHAPEL) with simple pointed windows. NICHOLSON'S FARM, a mid- to late C18 farmhouse, with dentilled eaves course and a first-floor band. Opposite on the W gable of ROSE COTTAGE are the initials R.A., said to be those of Richard Arkwright who purchased the Skerne estate in 1792. He was the son of Sir Richard Arkwright, patentee of the water-powered spinning frame. The Arkwrights rebuilt much of the village and surrounding farms in the early C19 including the typical hipped roofed three-bay farmhouses at SKERNE LEYS and GRANGE FARM.

(BELL MILLS,) ½ m. NW, a large mid-C20 brick flour mill replacing a four-storey brick watermill which had been built as a textile and carpet manufactory in 1792.

See also Wansford.

SKIDBY

0030

ST MICHAEL. There was a chapel at Skidby by 1225 and until 1859 it was part of Cottingham parish. The church, which stands on a raised mound, is a modest building with a rustic charm

This annotated page from *Yorkshire: York and the East Riding* (referred to as YER in this book) explains the abbreviations used in both books, and shows how *Looking at Buildings* complements the detailed descriptions in the *Buildings of England* series.

LANDSCAPE AND BUILDING MATERIALS

Before the C19 the appearance of buildings and their location was largely determined by the natural environment and in particular by the availability or otherwise of good building materials. In the East Riding there are five distinct regions ranging from the great curve of the chalk uplands, the Wolds, with dramatic coastal scenery where it meets the sea near Flamborough Head, to the low-lying Vale of York in the west. In between is the narrow strip of the Jurassic Hills, to the south-east is the Plain of Holderness and to the north the Vale of Pickering.

None of the five regions has good quality building stone, or had an abundant supply of timber in the Middle Ages. Only the most prestigious buildings, such as Beverley Minster and the principal East Riding churches, were constructed from imported stone: chiefly white magnesium limestone quarried near Tadcaster and floated in barges down the Ouse, Humber and other rivers close to the building sites. The limestone and sandstone of the Jurassic Hills, the chalk of the Wolds and the cobblestones collected from the fields and beaches of Holderness were used in village churches and domestic buildings. In some places use was made of stone plundered from local monastic sites after the Dissolution.

The East Riding did, however, have plentiful deposits of clay and by the early C14, Hull and Beverley became established centres of brickmaking. Until the mid C18 typical village houses and farm buildings had mud or chalk walls with some crude timber-framing, but from the late C17 to early C18 brickmaking became more widespread, with brickworks established by the great landowners. By the mid C19 there were some 80 brickyards in the riding and bricks were being exported to the expanding towns of the West Riding and further afield.

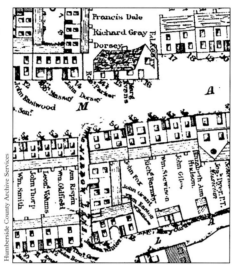

Just as the mud, timber and chalk walls of houses were replaced with a more durable building material, so the thatched roofs, common throughout the East Riding until the mid C18, were replaced with less inflammable material: usually the distinctive curved pantiles. These were imported from Holland in the C17, then made locally from the early C18. After the growth of the railways, slate imported from Wales became more common especially in the towns. A plan of Pocklington in 1855 shows only one building had a thatched roof, all the other buildings having pantile or slate roofs. By the late C19, urban buildings made use of a range of high-quality stone from the West Riding and further afield and still greater variety was provided by the use of terracotta and faience for decorative detail on public houses, shops, banks and schools.

LEFT: Extract from a plan of Pocklington of 1855 by William Watson, showing thatched house on Chapmangate.

RIGHT: The Wolds, looking south from the deserted village of Wharram Percy.

BELOW RIGHT: The chalk cliffs of Selwick Bay seen from Flamborough Head.

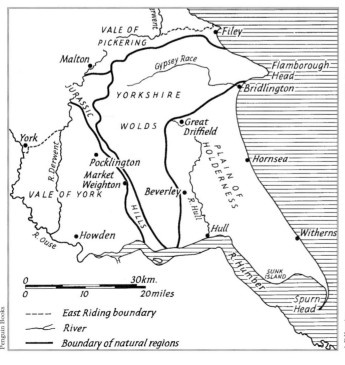

West End, Walkington, photographed c.1910. The cottage on the left with the thatched roof is typical of East Riding village housing before the C19.

Manor Farm, Fraisthorpe. An early-C19 cobble farm building with pantile roof and brick quoins.

Questions to consider

■ Explore a village or the older part of a town and discover the building materials used.

■ Which materials are from the locality and which have been imported?

■ How many types of brick bonds can you find? (see p.32, fig.1)

■ Have traditional materials been used for recent repairs or alterations?

■ What can old photographs and drawings tell you about the character of villages in the past?

Examples of building materials in the East Riding

Building materials	Characteristics	Location & examples of buildings
STONE		
Chalkstone	Great range in quality. Hard-wearing chalkstone quarried in NE Wolds, much of the rest weathers badly when exposed. Often whitewashed for protection. Some chalk walls faced in brick.	Used throughout the Wolds from Middle Ages. At Flamborough almost complete late C17 lighthouse of chalkstone.
Sandstone and Oolitic limestone	Best local building stone but rarely of a quality to produce a smooth ashlar finish or carved detail. Cream to rich brown in colour.	From the Jurassic belt. Used from the early Middle Ages for local churches and from C17 to early C19 for farmhouses, cottages and out-buildings in villages from e.g. South Cave in the south to Acklam in the north.
Cobble	Basalt cobbles widely used, some quite large. Great skill needed for building. Smaller brick-sized cobbles used in C19 often laid in herring-bone pattern. Last used for building in mid to late C19.	Use largely confined to south and east Holderness, except for urban street paving. 35 churches from Middle Ages to mid C19 at least partly cobble-built. C17 cobble cottages at Hornsea.
TIMBER	Scarcity of woodland in the E Riding by early Middle Ages. The few surviving timber-framed buildings, both cruck-framed and box-framed, are with one exception, insubstantial.	A few box-framed houses remain in the Vale of York and in and near Beverley. Substantial late-medieval aisled barn at Easington. Cruck-framed houses once more common on the Wolds e.g. at Octon.
CLAY		
'Mud'	Term used for the solid clay walled houses common throughout the region.	Only two remaining examples at Beeford and Roos.
Brick	Used for some prestigious buildings from the early C14, then for farm-houses and cottages from the early C18. Usually red or brown; white bricks used from late C18.	Throughout the region. Early brick buildings include Holy Trinity Church, Hull, North Bar, Beverley, and Watton Priory.
Pantiles	Distinctive orange tiles with double curve. Manufactured locally from early C18. Some blue-glazed pantiles e.g. at Burton Constable.	Replaced thatch throughout the E Riding from mid C18. Almost the only roofing material except in towns where slate was introduced by early C19.
THATCH	Until the mid C18 the universal roofing material in both town and country. Wheat or rye straw, sometimes reeds.	Only two authentic thatched buildings remain: the late medieval barn at Easington and an early C18 farmhouse at Howsham, both with renewed thatch.

Old Lighthouse, Flamborough. An octagonal four-storey chalkstone tower built 1674. After three centuries of exposure to the elements its good state of preservation demonstrates the durability of some chalkstone.

Oak Cottage, South Dalton. A rare survival of a C17 timber-framed house.

Elmswell Old Hall. A brick manor house built c.1635. The brick-mullioned windows in the gable end are original.

MEDIEVAL RUINS

Some of the earliest buildings in the East Riding are in ruins. This section focuses on two types of medieval buildings which were deliberately destroyed: castles and monasteries.

Castles

More than three hundred years separate the building of Skipsea and Wressle castles, an indication of the continuing unsettled nature of society in the Middle Ages. The design of the castles, however, shows considerable changes in castle building techniques and in the occupants' expectations of comfort and splendour as well as security. Both castles were ultimately destroyed for military reasons. King Henry III ordered the destruction of Skipsea Castle after its owner, William de Forz, Count of Aumale and Lord of Holderness, led a rebellion in 1221. What remains are the impressive earthworks of a motte-and-bailey castle built by Drogo de la Beuvriere, the first Lord of Holderness, soon after the Norman Conquest, when a rapidly built stronghold was essential protection for the invading Normans against a potentially hostile local population. The huge motte, some 11 metres high and 100 metres in diameter was originally an island in Skipsea mere until the land was drained in the C18. There is no trace of the timber keep built on top of the motte but a small section of cobble walling is visible on the south-east side. The bailey, or outer court, lies to the west on a crescent-shaped area of higher ground, protected by a high bank and a wide outer ditch.

Wressle Castle is the principal survivor in the East Riding of a major stone castle of the later Middle Ages. It was built by Sir Thomas Percy in about 1380 on the banks of the River Derwent, extended and altered over two centuries, and survived until the Civil War, when it was largely demolished by Parliamentarians in 1650 to prevent Royalists seizing it as their stronghold. The chief remains are two massive towers and the shell of a southern range between them. A drawing and plans from about 1600 show

that there were four stone ranges around a courtyard, with four corner towers, as at Bolton Castle in the North Riding. A fifth tower formed a tall gatehouse in the middle of the east range. The fine quality of the ashlar and the elaborate upper windows – no longer designed for defence – give a hint of what the castle was like in its heyday in the C15 and early C16 as one of the main residences of the Earls of Northumberland. By this time castles were valued for prestige as much as for defence.

ABOVE: Wressle Castle from the south. The interior of the southern range was gutted by fire in 1796.

RIGHT: Wressle Castle: view and ground plan based on originals of c.1600 at Petworth House.

1 Gatehouse
2 Chapel Tower
3 Constable Tower
4 Hall (on first floor)
5 Lord's Tower
6 Kitchen Tower
7 Bakehouse
8 Brew House

LEFT: Skipsea Castle is an example of a motte-and-bailey castle, the earliest type of castle in England.

BELOW: Reconstruction of how Skipsea Castle might have appeared c.1200.

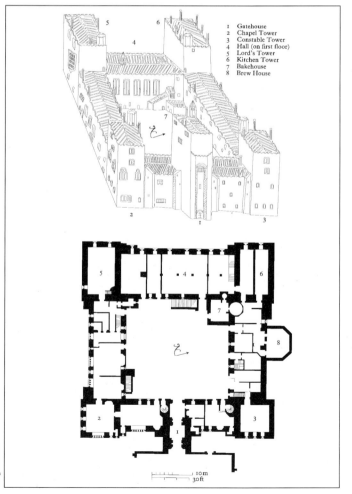

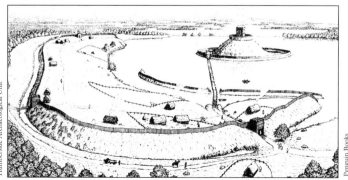

Monasteries

Monasteries were among the wealthiest establishments of the Middle Ages. As a result of bequests and other donations, they could afford extensive, regularly laid out stone buildings for both the church and the domestic needs of the monastic community. After the monasteries were abolished by Henry VIII, some of their buildings were converted to other uses, others were demolished. Many survived as ruins, and from the C18 became valued both for their picturesque appeal, and for the evidence they provided of the high artistic quality of medieval design.

Kirkham Priory was founded about 1125 by Walter Espec, Lord of Helmsley, for Augustinian Canons. The east part of the church, after its major rebuilding in the C13, became a favourite burying place of the Lords of Helmsley. The remains of the church itself are fragmentary, but some of the C13 east wall survives. Parts further west are older, suggesting that the money for the rebuilding must have run out. The arrangement of the domestic buildings shown on the plan were largely revealed by excavations. Little survives of these because, after the Priory had been suppressed on the orders of Henry VIII in 1539, the site was then plundered for building stone. However, enough of the gatehouse remains to appreciate its elaborate character.

BELOW: Kirkham Priory gatehouse. A combination of sculpture and elaborate tracery were key ingredients of the 'Decorated Gothic' of the late C13 and C14.

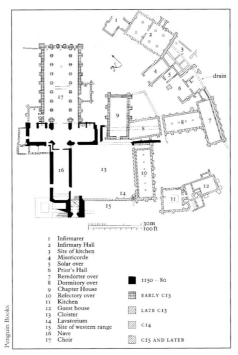

ABOVE: Plan of Kirkham Priory.

1	Infirmarer
2	Infirmary Hall
3	Site of kitchen
4	Misericorde
5	Solar over
6	Prior's Hall
7	Reredorter over
8	Dormitory over
9	Chapter House
10	Refectory over
11	Kitchen
12	Guest house
13	Cloister
14	Lavatorium
15	Site of western range
16	Nave
17	Choir

■ 1150 – 80
▦ EARLY C13
▨ LATE C13
▧ C14
▨ C15 AND LATER

'The outer façade has a wide arch of continuous mouldings with a crocketed gable running into the second stage. There is much sculpture: St George and the Dragon, David and Goliath l. and r. of the gable, and above, Christ in a pointed oval recess or vesica, with pellet decoration, and two more figures (St Bartholomew and St Philip) in niches. These last figures are between two upper windows with a trefoil of Kentish type, i.e. with spurs, set in a spherical triangle. The upper stage has five crocketed gables ... Between these, and elsewhere, is sumptuous heraldry including the arms of de Ros, Scrope and de Fortibus.'
(YER pp.589–90)

BELOW: Dominican Friary, Beverley.

Eddie Ryle-Hodges
Penguin Books
Humberside Archaeological Unit

Suggestions for looking at ruined sites

■ Study a ground plan to work out why the buildings were aligned in a particular way.

■ Compare similar buildings or sites to provide clues.

■ Examine the types of stones, which can show how a building was constructed: you may find rough stone used for foundations below ground, smoothly dressed stone used for wall surfaces and around openings, rubble used for thick walls (often between skins of dressed stone which have been taken for use elsewhere).

■ Search for evidence of how buildings protected their occupants, and their heating, lighting and water supply. How was food stored and cooked?

■ Check architectural details for different styles which may indicate several building phases.

■ Look for elaborate carving which may indicate the high status of the building or its users.

Questions to consider

■ Why should a ruined site be conserved and protected?

■ How should ruins be preserved – as picturesque remains covered in ivy? – repaired and roofed so that they can have a use? – consolidated, with excavated parts left visible?

■ Who should look after them?

■ How much information should be provided on site?

Skipsea Castle is open to the public; Wressle Castle is in private ownership and not open to visitors. Other monastic sites in the East Riding are Bridlington Priory (church adapted as a parish church), YER p.342, Watton Priory (C15 prior's house converted for domestic use after Dissolution), YER p.735, Beverley Friary (one building remains, restored as a Youth Hostel), YER p.301.

MEDIEVAL CHURCH DESIGN

The East Riding has some of England's finest churches dating from the C13 to the C14. Among them **Beverley Minster** is an outstanding example of medieval architecture. The Minster was a collegiate foundation (i.e. served by a college of priests) and comparable in size to a great abbey or cathedral. The grandeur of the building owes much to the cult of St John of Beverley (died in 721, canonized in 1037) whose shrine, placed above the reredos, was a centre of pilgrimage and place of sanctuary. The present Minster (successor to several earlier buildings) was begun about 1230 with work continuing on it for more than two hundred years. The long building period is demonstrated by the changes of style within the building.

Exterior
The west front with its ceremonial entrances is the showpiece of the exterior of a great medieval church. Often one of the last parts to be built, when money was running out, it was frequently not completed as intended. Beverley's two tower west front, probably completed at the very end of the C14, is a rare case of an entirely

consistent symmetrical composition in the Gothic Perpendicular style. An emphasis on vertical lines is achieved by the use of repetitive narrow rectangular surface panelling, enhancing the slimness of the towers. In contrast the ogee hoods of the main window and doorway are still in the tradition of the Decorated style of the C14.

'The towers have buttresses at the angles which step back substantially at the height of the sill of the bell-openings. They are panelled and have niches for images ... The bell openings are of three lights, tall, with a transom and panel tracery. Above them is blank panelling, and the towers end in fourteen pinnacles, the corner ones set diagonally.' (YER pp.286–7)

BELOW LEFT: The west front.

BELOW RIGHT: The east part of the Minster, containing the High Altar and Sanctuary, and the choir stalls for the clergy, was begun around 1230. The nave, just visible beyond the organ case, was not built until the C14. It continues the general design although the details change.

Surroundings and plan
The Minster, unlike some other great churches, does not have a close of related buildings. Originally it was less isolated, for there was a manor house belonging to the Archbishops of York near the south-west corner. (The Archbishops were the sole lords of Beverley until the Minster passed to the Crown in 1542.) There was also a chapter house to the north of the choir. This, no longer having a purpose, was demolished in 1550 after the college had been suppressed. Only its staircase remains. The building is aligned east to west, with the high altar at the eastern end and access for worshippers by the North Porch toward the western end. The two pairs of transepts, aligned north–south, provided space for additional altars.

Interior
The proportion of wall to opening, and the extent of decoration are important factors determining the character of the interior. As in many great churches, there are three tiers: the arcade opening to the aisles, a middle storey (or triforium), corre-

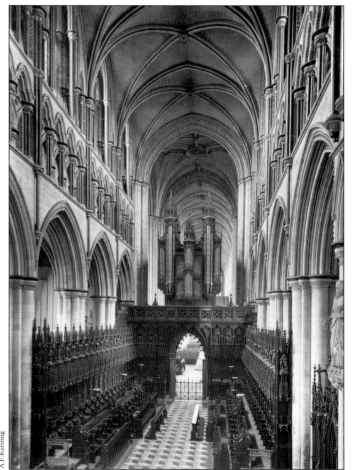

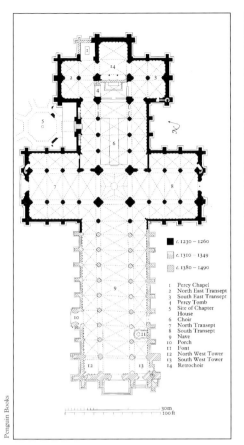

Plan of Beverley Minster.

View of Thornton's framed shoring.

Penguin Books

sponding to the aisle roof space, and the clerestory (or clear-storey) with windows rising above the aisle roofs. Between the arcade arches are wall shafts which rise to support the ribs of the main vault.

Characteristic C13 Gothic features are

■ thick arcade piers composed of clustered shafts

■ Purbeck marble for smaller shafts

■ moulded capitals

■ trefoil-headed arcading in the triforium

■ lancet windows in the clerestory.

Later changes

The north transept is a reminder of the care given to the building in the C18 when the transept was close to collapse. Following Nicholas Hawksmoor's survey of the Minster in 1716–17, a York architect, William Thornton, devised a great wooden frame to screw the north front back into place in 1719. The Minster was extensively restored at this time.

Building materials used at Beverley

■ oolitic limestone in the oldest part of the building at the eastern end

■ magnesian limestone for the bulk of the building

■ brick for the C14 nave vaulting

■ Purbeck marble from Dorset for shafting and arcading

Other churches to visit

At **Wharram-le-Street, Riccall, Newbald, Skerne** and **Stillingfleet** are churches with interesting Norman work. **St Augustine, Hedon,** is a large early-C13 church with a fine Perp crossing tower, **St Patrick, Patrington,** a beautiful church of the Dec period with a Perp spire. **Holy Trinity, Hull,** is a magnificent town church begun in the early C14, remarkable for its early use of brick, while **Beverley,** in addition to the Minster, has the impressive parish church of **St Mary,** dating mostly from the C14 and C15. YER gives details of all these and many more.

Questions to consider about Beverley Minster

■ How do the details of the Gothic interior compare with the west front?

■ How well have alterations made in the C18 and C19 blended with the medieval architecture?

■ How does the architecture reflect that the eastern end is the most sacred part of the Minster?

■ How well does the building suit modern forms of worship?

■ What conservation problems does the Minster present today?

ABOVE: St Patrick, Patrington.
LEFT: St. Mary, Beverley.
BELOW: St Augustine, Hedon.

MEDIEVAL CHURCHES: FURNISHINGS AND FITTINGS

Many fine pieces of craftsmanship were created to enhance the medieval church interior. This section focuses on the great variety of furnishings and fittings in stone, wood and metal.

Stone

Some of the earliest examples of stone carving are older than the churches in which they are now housed. Stone crosses, such as the fine example at Nunburnholme dating from around 1000, were carved with subjects proclaiming the Christian faith in a society still partly pagan. Among the most durable of church furnishings are fonts, traditionally placed near the western entrance to the church. On the Norman example at St Mary, Kirkburn, a band with religious subjects, including St Peter receiving two keys from Christ, is placed above a lower band with animals and patterns. In contrast, on the C14 font at Holy Trinity Church, Hull, the architectural forms of the concave gables rising from the underside up the bowl dominate the design.

Stone carving of the highest quality can be seen on the reredos (the screen behind the high altar) in Beverley Minster – 'one of the most luscious displays' of the Decorated style, which dates from c.1340. Its purpose was to carry the shrine of St John of Beverley. The Percy Tomb forms an integral part of the reredos. The ogee

LEFT: The Norman font at St Mary, Kirkburn: a *'jumble of delightful rustic carvings'.* (YER p.583)

RIGHT: The C14 font at Holy Trinity, Hull; *'very varied, close, with very lively carving all over e.g. angels with upfolded wings, leafage and in the sixteen quatrefoils, a huntsman, a boar's head, leopards' faces and fleurons.'* (YER p.508)

arches and cusping are embellished by a wealth of carved figures:

'a high ogee arch under a gable, the arch three-dimensional or nodding, ogee cusped and sub-cusped. The cusp ends are angels. In the largest spandrels of the cusping are splendid little figures in relief, seven knights in armour and a lady all with heraldry ... On splendid figure brackets, leaning out from the crockets l. and r., are pairs of angels, those to the aisle holding the Instruments of the Passion. The quality of these and of the two Christs is as fine as anything of the C14 in France or Germany.' (YER pp.290-1)

The influence of the carvers of the Percy Tomb can be seen in the

canopied tombs at Welwick, Bainton and Holy Trinity, Hull.

ABOVE: This misericord at St Mary, Beverley, shows a hunter, a wounded fox and an ape-doctor. Animals were often used to represent human characteristics. The fox symbolised cunning, the ape, seen as less than human, is equated here with a quack doctor.

Wood

Internal divisions within churches and seating for the clergy provided many opportunities for the woodcarver. The Ripon school of carvers, active in the early C16, may have been responsible for the particularly fine rood screen, (the screen dividing choir and chancel), at St Oswald, Flamborough. Earlier carving can be seen at St Mary, Beverley, where there are twenty-eight C15 misericords. These brackets on the underside of choir seats, designed to provide support for the occupant when standing, often portray secular and humorous subjects rather than religious themes.

The carving on this early cross shaft at St James, Nunburnholme, mixes the tradition of classical figure sculpture with Scandinavian-derived ornament.

LEFT: The C14 tomb to a member of the Percy family at Beverley Minster, *'the most splendid of all British Dec funerary monuments'.*

Metal

One of the most remarkable examples of C12 ironwork is that decorating one of the original doors at Stillingfleet.

'It has large C-shaped hinges and among other motifs the figures of a man and a woman, an interlocked cross, a strip of interlace, a single figure and a ship with a distinctly Viking character with a serpent terminal and steerboard.' (YER p.712)

The skill of the medieval metal worker is displayed in monumental brasses which, by the C15, were some of the more common forms of memorial, the majority in the East Riding being made in York workshops. Less expensive than stone memorials, brasses became popular among a wider range of people. Figures include knights in armour and their wives (Brandesburton, 1397, and Harpham, 1418) and priests (Bainton, 1429, and Beeford, 1472).

ABOVE: The C12 door at St Helen, Stillingfleet. The human figures have been interpreted as Adam and Eve and the ship as Noah's Ark.

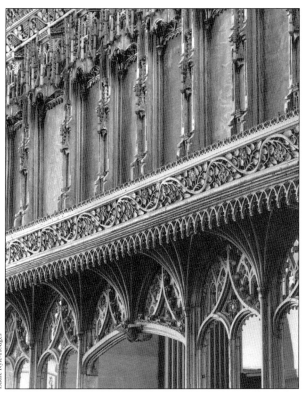

LEFT: The intricately carved parapet of the rood screen at St Oswald, Flamborough, has fifteen canopied niches for paintings. Originally the whole screen was painted.

This brass is one of several monuments to the St Quintin family at St John of Beverley, Harpham. It shows Sir Thomas de St Quintin and his wife beneath a Gothic canopy, with heraldic shields above identifying their families. Sir Thomas, who died in 1418, is shown in the plate armour of the period. The lion and dogs at their feet, symbolising courage and fidelity, often appear on brasses.

Questions to consider

■ What changes in the stone masons' skills are evident between the Norman and Decorated styles?

■ What types of religious and secular themes were used as decoration?

■ How are architectural styles reflected in furnishings and fittings?

■ How does the material used affect the nature of the carving?

Materials used for tombs

Stones with fine surfaces resembling marble were highly prized for carving and were sometimes brought from far afield

STONE	TOMB	CHURCH	DATE
Purbeck marble (from Dorset)	Knight in armour	Welton	c.1250–75
Frosterley marble (probably from County Durham)	Bishop Kirkham	Howden	1260
Alabaster (from Derbyshire)	Hilton family	Swine	1370–1410

Places to visit

YER gives details of numerous churches with rewarding medieval fittings and monuments; the most notable are mentioned on pp.43–7 of the Introduction. **Beverley Minster** has outstanding stalls and misericords of the early C16; the best collection of monuments is at **St Mary, Swine.**

THE JACOBEAN GREAT HOUSE

Burton Agnes Hall provides one of the most perfect examples of Jacobean architecture. The days when security needed to be given priority, as was the case when the nearby Burton Agnes Manor House was built in the C12, were long past. The estate eventually passed from the Stutvilles who built the Manor House, to the Griffiths in 1355. It was Sir Henry Griffith, then living in Staffordshire, who decided to build the Hall on his Yorkshire estate, probably following his appointment to serve on the Council of the North at York in 1599. Burton Agnes Hall was built between 1601 and 1610, dates which appear above the entrance doorway and on the gatehouse. There are four features of the Hall which together reflect the nature of Jacobean style and subsequent alterations to the Hall. These same features are useful in analysing the style of any great house.

Entrance to the grounds
Guests of Sir Henry approached his home past a three-storey gatehouse which signals the splendours to come:

'It has four octagonal turrets with ogee caps, two-light windows, and to the outside a wide arch of stone with wide two-bay blank arcading of stone to l. and r. Above are carved the arms of James I flanked by two allegorical figures. Sir Henry was fond of allegorical figures. The inner side of the gatehouse is plainer. It has instead of a coat of arms a four-light window.'
(YER p.368)

Entrance front
The symmetrical south front with its great bow windows is almost certainly the work of the Elizabethan architect, Robert Smythson (c.1535–1614), whose plan for the house survives.

'The bows with their ten-light mullioned and transomed windows are three storeys high. The centre of the house, where the windows were sashed c.1725, appears to be of three storeys plus attics, but here the small horizontal first-floor windows provide extra light for the Great Hall. The centre consists of a recessed plane with two oblong bays projecting from it and crowned by stone strapwork. The entrance is oddly tucked away in the l. of one of these projections, facing not S but E.' (YER p.368)

Floor plan
Behind the symmetry of the entrance front, the plan of the rooms reveals that some of the older traditions have been retained. On the ground floor, there is a Great Hall whose screen has two openings leading to the entrance

ABOVE: Burton Agnes gatehouse.

BELOW: Burton Agnes ground-floor plan.

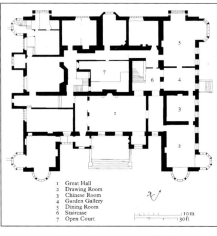

1 Great Hall
2 Drawing Room
3 Chinese Room
4 Garden Gallery
5 Dining Room
6 Staircase
7 Open Court

10 m
30 ft

ABOVE: Burton Agnes staircase.

passage and service rooms. Other rooms provide space for dining and social activities, once the function of the Great Hall in medieval buildings. The use of upstairs rooms for social functions encouraged the development of the grand stair. The splendid exam-

ple at Burton Agnes rises to the Long Gallery on the second floor, sited above the hall. Galleries were popular in Elizabethan great houses, as places of indoor recreation, but went out of favour in the late C17. At Burton Agnes the space was subdivided but restored to its original form in the C20.

Interior decoration
The lofty Great Hall with its screen next to the entrance passage continues medieval traditions, but the impact of the Italian Renaissance is seen in the incorporation of classical detail in both screen and chimneypiece, both

BELOW: Burton Agnes entrance front.

ABOVE: A detail of the Great Hall screen: St Mark and his symbol, a winged lion.

ABOVE: The Long Gallery drawn by C.J. Richardson in the mid C19. The elaborate free-flowing design of the plasterwork of the barrel vaulted ceiling is typical of the early C17. The centre panels of the chimneypiece are now in the Dining Room.

BELOW: Burton Agnes Great Hall.

Questions to consider

■ What characteristics of building design became possible once security was no longer an over-riding consideration?

■ How does the decoration of the gatehouse compare with that at Kirkham Priory? (see p.7)

■ Do the alterations made by different generations of owners harmonise with the whole?

■ How did planning and arrangement of rooms reinforce the status of the owner or their occupants?

■ How many different craft skills are represented by the furnishings and fittings in any of the main rooms?

crazily overcrowded, but one of the glories of Burton Agnes. The mixture of secular and religious themes is typical of the time.

The screen is of wood with pairs of Ionic columns flanking two highly decorated arches and supporting a small-scale frieze with figures of the twelve sons of Jacob who became the founding fathers of the Twelve Tribes of Israel. Above in the elaborate three-tiered plaster frieze the main figures in the first tier are the four Evangelists with their symbols. In the second tier are the twelve Apostles and above there are various scenes with angels, knights in armour and women in Elizabethan dress. The alabaster over-mantel of the chimneypiece shows the Parable of the Wise and Foolish Virgins.

...the front looks very uniform with severall round buildings on each side answerring each other, with Compass windows, and the middle is a round building and the door enters in in the side of that tower which was the old fashion in building...there is a noble gallery over all with large windows on the sides, and at each end painted very curiously, out of which you view the whole Country round, and discover the shipps under saile though at a good distance; the Gardens are large and are capable of being made very fine, they now remaine in the old fashion; there is one walke all the length of the Garden called the Crooked Walke, of grass well cutt and rowled, it is indented in and out in corners and so is the wall, which makes you thinke you are at the end off the walke severall tymes before you are, by means of the Codling hedge that is on the other side, this leads you to a Summer house that also opens to a large gravell walke that runns the breadth of the garden to the house ward.

Celia Fiennes, 1697

Gardens
The original layout of the gardens was still evident when Celia Fiennes visited the house in 1697. They have been altered since, but formal elements were re-introduced in the 1960s–80s.

For further details of Burton Agnes Hall see YER pp.366–71.
The house is open to the public.

ABOVE: Burton Constable Hall.

Other notable houses of the Elizabethan and Jacobean periods in the East Riding (all with later interiors): **Burton Constable Hall**, YER pp.361–77, open to the public; **Howsham Hall**, YER pp.494–5, now a school, and **Boynton Hall**, YER pp.334–6, a private house. Compare Burton Agnes Hall with the adjoining medieval manor house (English Heritage) and **Sledmere House**, on the following pages (both are open to the public).

THE COUNTRY HOUSE AND ITS SETTING

Sledmere

The Sykes family, owners of Sledmere since the mid C18, became the East Riding's greatest landowners by the later C19. Their country house and estate at Sledmere provide a striking example of the impact one family can have on the local environment over two centuries.

The house

Sledmere is a large H-shaped house in a restrained classical style. The south front is of three widely spaced bays with large tripartite windows of the type popular in the late C18. They are framed by blind segmental or semi-circular arches containing decorative Coade-stone panels. The house was gutted by fire in 1911. A decision then had to be made whether to restore the building or design a new house. Mark Sykes acting on behalf of his elderly father, Sir Tatton II, clashed with the architect, Walter Brierley of York, who favoured a new design. In the end the family's preference for restoration determined the outcome, and although the interior was substantially altered and the west front redesigned, the present house is largely a copy of the late C18 building.

Sir Tatton Sykes

ABOVE:
Sir Christopher and Lady Sykes by George Romney.
RIGHT: Sledmere House from the south-west.
BELOW: Sledmere from the north-east, 1987. The new road of the late 1770s sweeps round to the north of Sledmere House and the church. The octagonal kitchen garden and the estate housing are clearly visible.
BOTTOM: Sledmere, sites of the old and the new village.

A.F.Kersting

Richard Morris

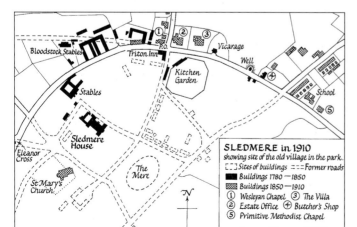

The Sykes family and Sledmere

Richard Sykes 1706–61	Hull merchant, inherited estate in 1748. Began building Sledmere House and stables 1751. Rebuilt church 1758 and removed part of the village to the south of the house hiding the rest by avenues of trees.
Sir Christopher Sykes 2nd baronet 1749–1801	Took over estate 1776. Greatly enlarged the house 1783–1800. Refronted the stables. Landscaped the park and removed the remaining village houses. He resited the York to Bridlington road to the north of the house erecting vicarage, shop and inn, along it. He designed the farmhouses built in the newly enclosed fields and planted 1,000 acres of trees.
Sir Tatton Sykes I 4th baronet 1772–1863	Inherited from brother in 1823. Built the bloodstock stables 1830 and the cupola over the village well 1840.
Sir Tatton Sykes II 5th baronet 1826–1913	Completed the village, building school and school house 1874–5, semi-detached and terraced estate cottages in 1860s–80s, post office, estate office, and houses for the forester and clerk-of-works in 1890s. He rebuilt the church 1893–8, erected the Eleanor Cross 1896–8, and provided sites for two Methodist chapels.
Sir Mark Sykes 6th baronet 1879–1919	Rebuilt and enlarged house after the 1911 fire. Designed the Waggoners' Memorial and built two pairs of cottages.
Sir Richard Sykes 7th baronet 1905–78	Pulled down the early-twentieth-century north wing of the house using materials for constructing a square of neo-Georgian estate houses, 1946. Opened house to public.
Sir Tatton Sykes III 8th baronet	Has carried out much restoration and refurbishment on house and estate, including Library, 1979–81.

SLEDMERE in 1910
showing site of the old village in the park.
Sites of buildings === Former roads
■ Buildings 1780 – 1850
▨ Buildings 1850 – 1910
① Wesleyan Chapel ③ The Villa
② Estate Office ⊕ Butcher's Shop
⑤ Primitive Methodist Chapel

0   100   200 yards
0   100   200 metres

Bloodstock Stables
Triton Inn
Vicarage
Well
Kitchen Garden
Stables
School
Sledmere House
Eleanor Cross
St Mary's Church
The Mere

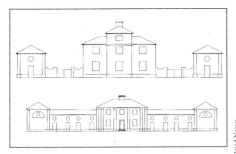

Marramatte and Life Hill Farms, built 1778. Elevations attributed to Sir Christopher Sykes.

Sledmere school and schoolhouse, 1874–5 by G.E. Street.

Questions to consider

■ How would you have rebuilt Sledmere House in 1911?

■ What is your opinion of the church?

■ How do the estate houses differ in design, material and size?

The landscape

The mid-C18 house stood in modest grounds with a large village sited prominently to the south. In a number of stages the settlement was totally removed, the open arable fields enclosed and the village roads closed or re-routed. The magnificent landscape created by Sir Christopher Sykes, with advice from Capability Brown, has a series of farmsteads which he designed both to serve the newly enclosed farmland and to provide eyecatchers from the house. These are the Gothick Castle Farm to the east, and the classical Life Hill Farm and Marramatte Farm to the south and west respectively.

The village

Sledmere is an excellent example of an estate village designed to complement the house and park. Following the destruction of the old village, a few key buildings were erected in the 1780s and others followed in the C19. It was Sir Tatton II who completed the village in the last quarter of the C19. He engaged John Birch, who specialised in estate buildings, to design a great range of housing. Pairs of typical estate cottages, gabled with tiled roofs sloping down over porches, set back in sizeable gardens, contrast with very urban looking terraces with only small yards behind. In the 1890s Birch designed a fine group of more substan-

Estate cottages, Croom Lane, Sledmere. A variation of John Birch's design for a pair of agricultural labourers' cottages awarded a prize by the Society of Arts in 1864.

St Mary's church, Sledmere, 1893–8 by Temple Moore. The base of the tower is medieval.

Rear of terrace of ten cottages, Bridlington Road, Sledmere. This late C19 estate housing is surprisingly urban in appearance.

A rotunda of Tuscan columns with a lead-covered dome erected over Sledmere village well in 1840. It bears an inscription recording the achievements of Sir Christopher Sykes 'in building and planting and inclosing on the Yorkshire Wolds'.

The church

As part of the improvements to the setting of the house, the village church was rebuilt in 1758 with the exception of the medieval tower. The nave and chancel were rebuilt again in 1893–8 in the Decorated style for Sir Tatton Sykes II, who had already rebuilt seven churches on the estate. (See pp.18–19 on C19 churches and chapels.) Whereas the classical style was favoured for the rebuilt house, the Gothic style was preferred for the church. The exterior is of Whitby stone, the interior of red sandstone. The craftsmanship throughout is of the highest quality. Pevsner in 1972 called the church 'large, quite perfect, and patently dull', but also quoted the architectural historian Goodhart Rendell's view that it was 'perhaps one of the loveliest churches of England', and commented 'to such an extent can reactions differ'.

tial red-brick buildings whose details are in a 'Domestic Tudor' style: *'Gabled, with flat-tile roofs, four-centred-arched doorways and mullioned windows with moulded surrounds, occasional hoodmoulds, bargeboards and tall octagonal stacks.'*

The Villa, Sledmere. Built for the clerk of works, 1898 to the designs of John Birch.

Sledmere is described in YER pp. 691–9. The house and grounds are open in the summer months. **Sewerby Hall**, YER pp.678–9, is also accessible. Descriptions of other great eighteenth- and nineteenth-century country houses of the East Riding not open to the public, will be found in YER: **Birdsall House**, pp.326–7; **Everingham Hall**, pp.412–3; **Grimston Garth**, pp.445–7; **Houghton Hall**, pp.667–9; and **Scampston Hall**, pp.669–71.

COUNTY TOWN

The predominant character of **Beverley** is that of a Georgian county town. Beverley has fulfilled the role of administrative centre of the East Riding since the early C18. By then quarter sessions of the Justices of the Peace for the riding were held here, and the town was attracting the county gentry and their families along with lawyers, doctors and craftsmen. Their C18 houses now complement the older landmarks of the Minster and St Mary's church, which reflect the town's earlier importance as a centre of pilgrimage and trade in the Middle Ages.

Market and shops

The handsome Market Cross, erected in the large Saturday Market in 1711–14, provided shelter for traders with their perishable goods. It also demonstrated the civic pride of a parliamentary borough and bears the arms of the borough, the crown and the two MPs, Sir Charles Hotham and Sir Michael Warton. The design makes bold use of classical forms, applying the early C18 Baroque style to a traditional form of Market Cross.

'It is an extremely successful version of the traditional type of open shelter, square with canted corners and eight Roman Doric columns supporting the four diagonals in pairs. It has a full entablature with triglyphs and guttae and eight vases as pinnacles. The jolly cupola roof of fanciful outline is topped by a square glazed lantern which in turn is surmounted by an obelisk and weathervane.' (YER p.305)

BELOW: The Market Cross.

RIGHT: Court Room ceiling, the Guildhall.

BELOW RIGHT: The Beverley Arms.

There are several examples of Georgian shops not far from the Market Cross. On the east side of Saturday Market there is a row of mainly mid-C18 brick and pantile shops. The least altered one is No. 28, 'a narrow three-storey shop of c.1765 with wood modillion eaves cornice, a late-C18 canted bay, a canopy over door and window and a tripartite sash to the first floor'. No. 14 Norwood still has a late Georgian shopfront with a large bow window.

Inns

Beverley's inns and alehouses were centres for trade, administration and social life. Two inns on North Bar Within vied for the position of main meeting place for the town and the riding. The Beverley Arms Hotel was rebuilt in 1794–6 as 'the premier inn of the East Riding' and given its new

name, grander sounding than the former 'The Blue Bell'. It has a neat brick façade of three storeys with a parapet. The stone entrance portico has an iron balcony above reached from a round-headed first-floor window. Here the successful parliamentary candidates for the town were presented. The three bays on the left are an extension of 1966–7. Further along the street, Nos. 41–47, an eleven-bay block, was the former Tiger Inn, the chief rival to the Beverley Arms, built c.1740.

Administrative buildings

Although inns could be used for some administrative purposes, the formal meetings of the corporation of the borough were held in the Guildhall in Register Square. The façade was rebuilt in 1832–5 in the form of a large Greek Doric portico with a triglyph frieze and pediment. Behind is the remnant of a late medieval timber-framed building, and the court room and council chamber, built by Beverley's foremost builder–architect, William Middleton, in 1762. The room retains many of its original furnishings and fittings including an impressive Rococo plaster ceiling, at the centre of which is the seated figure of Justice, shown in flowing robes as though floating on a cloud.

Another symbolic figure of Justice, this time standing in a more statuesque pose, surmounts the former East Riding Sessions House built in New Walk in 1805–10. Designed by Charles Watson of Wakefield, this classical grey-brick building is in the severe Grecian style popular in the early C19:

'three-bay, two-storey centre block with arched first-floor windows fronted by a large Greek Ionic stone portico with

four unfluted columns and a pediment. Royal Arms in pediment and a figure of Justice in Coade stone above. Low single-storey wings to l. and r.' (YER p.303)

Leisure

North of the town, a tree-lined walk, New Walk, was laid out in the 1780s by the corporation, a promenade being a popular feature in Georgian towns. From the late 1820s it was lit by gas and the original lamp standards survive on the west side. Although built up with houses during the C19, New Walk retains its trees. It is a precious survival, as evidence for other Georgian leisure activities have disappeared. There was a theatre from c.1755–76 at Nos. 90–92 Walkergate. Part of the wall of a later Georgian

The Sessions House.

New Walk c.1840, looking south from the Sessions House to North Bar.

theatre survives on the west side of Lairgate at the corner of Champney Road. The Assembly Rooms, built in Norwood 1761–3 and a grandstand for horse racing built on the Hurn pasture 1767–8, both designed by John Carr, were demolished between the two World Wars.

Houses

Georgian Beverley has many grand houses, some still set in the remnants of their once extensive grounds. As the centre of public life and county society, the great landowners such as the

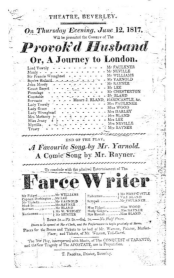

1817 Playbill for the theatre in Lairgate, built 1817, closed 1840.

Questions to consider

■ The classical tradition derived from Roman and Greek architecture is basic to much building of the Georgian period, but could be interpreted in many different ways. How were classical features used in the C18 and early C19? (For drawings of classical details see p.33.)

■ How and why did public and domestic buildings differ in their exterior design?

■ What problems are caused for a modern community by having so many historic buildings in the town centre? What are the benefits?

■ How well have C20 buildings blended with earlier ones? (See also p.30.)

■ Georgian lamps survive on New Walk. Has other street furniture been designed in keeping with surrounding buildings?

■ Using a Trade Directory from the past century, find out what trades were undertaken in one of the town streets you have visited.

Hotham, Pennyman, Strickland, Sykes and Warton families had their town houses here. The Sykes' house was at No. 62 North Bar Without – an attractive two-storey red-brick building of the 1730s. The wealth of small-town lawyers was demonstrated by their houses. No. 7 Hengate was built for one, Henry Spendlove, in 1708–9, and has the characteristic Beverley four-bay façade with off-centre entrance. Its pedimented doorcase with Doric columns was added c.1785. Another lawyer, Jonathan Midgley, built Norwood House around 1760 possibly to the designs of the York architect, Thomas Atkinson. Considered Beverley's best Georgian house, it has three storeys and five bays linked to low projecting wings.

'The main front has a pediment right across with a round window in an elaborate wooden Rococo cartouche with trailing chains of husks to l. and r. The first-floor windows have floating cornices and false balconies. The ground floor is rusticated with a prominent entrance doorway with a Gibbs surround. The rustication is vermiculated.' (YER p.308)

Other Georgian houses can be seen, for example, in Highgate, Keldgate and Newbegin ('a delightful Georgian backwater').

Georgian street lamp, North Bar Without.

LEFT: Norwood House.

VICTORIAN CHURCHES AND CHAPELS

Anglican churches

The C19 was a great period of church building and restoration or reconstruction of medieval churches in the East Riding. This rebuilding reflects the revival of the Anglican church partly in response to the growth of Nonconformity. Many of the surviving C19 churches were built in rural areas where the great landowners were generous benefactors. The towns too saw much church building. Hull alone had twenty new Anglican churches, but of these only three remain. Where medieval churches were badly in need of repair, opportunities were sometimes taken to 'improve' on what existed, with architects and craftsmen drawing enthusiastically on medieval sources. Although local architects designed some of the new or restored churches, the majority, and the best, were designed by leading national architects. The table provides some examples of their work.

One of the many medieval churches to be reconstructed was St Michael, Garton-on-the-Wolds. The original church was granted to Kirkham Priory in 1121 and probably rebuilt shortly afterwards. Sir Tatton Sykes I (see pp.14-15) funded the reconstruction by J.L. Pearson in 1856–7. The exceptional Victorian interior with its furnishings, stained glass and wall paintings dates from after 1872 when Sir Tatton Sykes II employed G.E. Street in place of Pearson. When Sir Nikolaus Pevsner visited the church one hundred years later the paintings were dirty and decaying. His comment 'it is essential that they be preserved' inspired the Pevsner Memorial Trust to put in hand a thorough cleaning and conservation programme in 1986–91.

Eddie Ryle-Hodges

LEFT: Street was eclectic in his use of medieval sources, attracted by bold and simple Early Gothic forms. At Howsham he combined these with an Italian inspired open porch and a decorative turret to make an effective and original composition.

BELOW : The wall paintings at St Michael, Garton-on-the-Wolds, by the eminent London firm of Clayton and Bell, cover every available surface. Oil and resin-bound pigments were painted on to primed plaster or stone to illustrate subjects ranging from severe Old Testament themes to the Labours of the Months and the Last Judgement. These details shows the killing of Cain, from the story of the Creation.

RCHME

A.F. Kersting

Pearson's exceptionally sumptuous church at South Dalton, with its noble tower and spire, transepts and aisled choir, is inspired by the pure Geometric, or Middle Pointed Gothic of the C13.

Some new rural Anglican churches				
Architect	**Benefactor**	**Church**	**Date**	**Predominant style**
J.L. Pearson	James Hall	St Leonard Scorborough	1857–9	Early English
J.L. Pearson	Lord Hotham	St Mary South Dalton	1858–61	Geometric
G.E. Street	Hannah Cholmley	St John Howsham	1859–60	Geometric
G.E. Street	Sir Tatton Sykes II	St Mary Wansford	1866–8	Geometric
G.E. Street	Sir Tatton Sykes II	St Mary Fimber	1869–71	Geometric
G.E. Street	Sir Tatton Sykes II	St Peter Helperthorpe	1871–3	Geometric
T.L. Moore	Sir Tatton Sykes II	St Mary Sledmere	1893–8	Decorated

The Chapel of the Virgin and St Everilda, Everingham, 1836–9, is an unusually sumptuous example of a Roman Catholic Chapel in the Italian manner.

Roman Catholic churches

Some of the East Riding's main landowning families were Roman Catholic. Following the Act of Emancipation in 1829 they were free to build churches once more. At Burton Constable Hall the Constable family converted the billiard room into a chapel in 1830 and at Everingham, another, unrelated, Constable family built the impressive chapel of the Virgin and St Everilda in 1836–9. Designed by an Italian architect Agostino Giorgioli, and adapted by John Harper of York, this 'alien and magnificent piece of architecture' celebrates the new found freedom. The Italian influence is evident in the basilican plan as well as several elements of the decoration.

'The interior is spectacular. The painting and gilding by J.F. Brown & Son of York cost over £1,100. White-and-gold coffered tunnel-vault with penetrations, coffered apse with a semi-circular (half-Pantheon) glazed skylight, and a coffered narrow W bay with sky-light for the organ gallery. All along the sides is an alternation of brown giant Corinthian scagliola columns and niches with marble statues of the Apostles (1839–44) by Luigi Bozzoni of Carrara. By him also the relief panels above the niches. The apse has giant pilasters and also statues in niches (the Virgin and three Saints) and the nave is separated from the apse by projecting square pillars.' (YER p.412)

RIGHT: Wallingfen Methodist Church at Newport, built in 1814, with its simple brick front and Gothic glazing, is Georgian chapel design at its most appealing.

Burlington Methodist Church at Bridlington, built 1884. This large and exotic urban chapel, in an Italianate style with rather Indian-looking turrets, illustrates the eclectic mixture of styles of the later C19.

Methodist chapels

The C19 saw a great expansion in Nonconformity. The Methodists were particularly strong in the East Riding. In 1851 the national Religious Census showed that the East Riding was second only to Cornwall in the percentage of attendances at Methodist chapels. Well over a hundred of the East Riding's villages had both a Wesleyan and a Primitive Methodist chapel by the second half of the C19. Only closed estate villages such as Londesborough or Escrick were without a chapel. Hull also was a hot-bed of Nonconformity, with some eighty

Questions to consider

■ Why did Gothic seem an appropriate style for many religious buildings in the C19?

■ Which aspects of the Gothic style were popular in the Victorian period?

■ How can Victorian buildings and their decoration be distinguished from medieval work?

■ How sympathetic were the Victorians to the medieval buildings which they restored?

■ Through using old directories and guide books, find out how many places of worship existed in a town or village a hundred years ago. How many are still standing?

Nonconformist chapels and meeting houses in 1881, of which eight remain. By the late C19 the urban chapels, with their meeting rooms and classrooms, were important social and educational centres.

Chapel design

Early Victorian chapels were little different from their Georgian predecessors – simple brick boxes with perhaps round-headed or occasionally Gothic windows with sashes and glazing bars. From the 1850s more elaborate Gothic and Italianate chapels were built. The Wesleyans and older Dissenters favoured the Gothic, and Primitive Methodists preferred Italianate.

THE RURAL SCENE 1750–1900

White House Farm, Scorborough. A modest early C18 farmhouse; one-storeyed with attics, of whitewashed brick and pantile.

Agriculture

Between the mid C18 and the mid C19 the rural landscape of the East Riding was transformed when the remaining large open arable fields and commons, still farmed on the medieval system, were enclosed. Parliamentary enclosure, particularly on the Wolds, resulted in a regular pattern of rectangular hedged fields, long straight roads with wide verges and large new farmsteads protected by plantations sited well away from the villages. The new two-storey end-stack farmhouses serving farms of up to 1,000 acres replaced the modest one-and-a-half storey village farmhouses from which the farmer, and his family, had worked as little as 50–100 acres. Young men and women hired by the year provided the workforce of the new farms and they were accommodated within the farmhouse, either in a rear wing or in an additional bay adjoining the main house.

ABOVE RIGHT: Early C19 warehouses at River Head, Great Driffield.

RIGHT: Lockington, Rectory Farm, an early C19 farmstead with two-storey end-stack farmhouse, hipped roof, and double foldyard.

ABOVE: Manor Farm, Ruston Parva, a two-storeyed post-enclosure farmhouse. This example was built soon after the enclosure of the open fields in 1805. The three-bay end-stack farmhouse has a near-contemporary fourth bay added to accommodate men living-in.

RIGHT: Sancton Hill Farm, Sancton, an ambitious model farm of 1858–62, illustrated in J.B. Denton's *Farm Homesteads of England*, 1864.

Despite the scale of the Georgian post-enclosure farmsteads few rivalled the ambitious steam-powered farms built at Enholmes, Patrington, in 1849 by William Marshall of Leeds, and Sancton Hill, Sancton, in 1858–62 by John Wells. The latter has been largely demolished but at Enholmes much remains including the vast five-fingered cattle shed through which a railway ran to deliver food and take away manure.

Communications

Improvement in communications began with the turnpiking of the road between Hull and Beverley in 1744. Within the next fifty years many main routeways across the riding were turnpiked. New road surfaces were laid and toll bars and milestones erected. Bridges were rebuilt or provided for the first time, as in 1792–3 at Bubwith, across the River Derwent, and Selby, across the River Ouse.

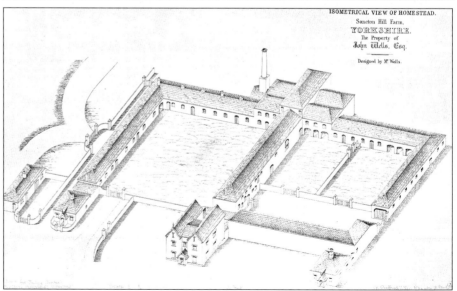

ISOMETRICAL VIEW OF HOMESTEAD.
Sancton Hill Farm,
YORKSHIRE.
The Property of
John Wells, Esq.

Designed by Mr Wells.

The unusually grand riverside building at Naburn Lock was built as a Banqueting House in 1824–5 for the Lord Mayor and Corporation of York, Trustees of the Ouse Navigation.

The navigation of these two rivers was improved by the building of locks in the C18. In 1824–5 the Lord Mayor and Corporation of York as trustees of the Ouse Navigation built a grand Banqueting House alongside Naburn Lock. Of the purpose-built canals the most successful was the Driffield Navigation, opened 1770, which provided a link, via the River Hull, between the rapidly developing corn-growing district of the Wolds and Hull and the expanding West Riding. River Head, Driffield, has an excellent group of late-C18 and early-C19 warehouses and mid-C19 cranes. Along the Pocklington Canal of 1815–19 is an attractive series of ramped brick bridges with rounded buttresses and curving parapets.

The former station at Skipwith, built in 1911.

Railways came to the East Riding in the 1840s and although most lines are now closed the former stations and other structures are scattered throughout the countryside. Most impressive is the railway viaduct built in 1846–7 at Stamford Bridge, over the River Derwent for the York–Market Weighton line. Less usual are the circular brick towers which top the air-shafts of the Drewton Tunnel, a great feat of engineering built 1881–3 along the Hull and Barnsley line. Railway stations range from the impressive series designed in the 1840s by the York architect, G.T. Andrews, along the lines from York to Market Weighton, York to Scarborough and Hull to Bridlington, to the simple half-timbered pavilions erected along the Derwent Valley Light Railway in 1911–12.

Air shaft for the Drewton tunnel, between Little Weighton and South Cave.

Rural Industry

'Fortunately for this district [East Riding], it is nearly as possible exempt from manufactories, ... it may indeed be looked upon as purely agricultural: perhaps there is not another in the kingdom of equal extent more completely of that description.'
(H.E. Strickland, *Agriculture of the East Riding of Yorkshire*, 1812.)

What little industry was to be found in the market towns and villages was largely concerned with processing agricultural produce. Flour milling was the most widespread industry, with some 60 water mills and 170 windmills in the East Riding in the early 1850s. Just over half the water-mill buildings survive, because they are attached to occupied mill-houses, and parts of at least 40 windmills – all tower mills. Attempts were made in the later C18 to establish a textile industry based on large-scale water mills at Driffield, Boynton and Wansford. The last, a carpet manufactory, opened in the 1790s, was owned by Sir Christopher Sykes of Sledmere. Wansford Mill stood on an island between the

Questions to consider

■ In what ways do post-enclosure farmhouses and farm buildings differ from the older village farmsteads?

■ What types of buildings exist at the heads of canals or river navigations?

■ To what present day uses can redundant mill buildings, Victorian railway stations and disused clay pits be put?

Driffield Canal and the River Hull, and employed some 400 men, women and children. It closed in the 1820s and the main buildings were demolished in the early C20 leaving only associated outbuildings. The small village water mill survives nearby.

The great explosion in building in town and countryside from the late C18 led to increased demand for bricks and pantiles. This demand was met largely by the many rural brick-yards and in particular by the establishment of the brickmaking community at Newport. Here at the junction of the Market Weighton canal, dug 1772–7, and the turnpike road running westward from Hull via South Cave, good brick-making clay was discovered and an industrial settlement grew up. Nothing now remains but water-filled clay pits.

ABOVE: The late-C18 water mill at Wansford. LEFT: Skidby Windmill, the only working windmill remaining in the East Riding, built in 1821 by Robert Garton, millwright, of Beverley.

Places to visit

Yorkshire Farming Museum, Murton near York; **Skidby Mill** is open to the public; **Stamford Bridge water mill** is now a restaurant. Most of the canals have public footpaths alongside and stretches of former railway lines, particularly those running from Beverley to Market Weighton, Market Weighton to Selby, and Hull to Hornsea have been made accessible as long-distance walks.

SEASIDE RESORTS

Although the small ports and fishing villages of the East Yorkshire coast, particularly Bridlington, Filey and Hornsea, had been attracting visitors for sea bathing from the later C18, it was not until the arrival of the railway in the mid C19 that they became popular resorts. It was, indeed, a railway company that created Withernsea. The differing fortunes experienced in the development of Filey, Bridlington and Withernsea, partly accounted for by their physical setting, have produced contrasting architecture.

Filey's picturesque bay, bounded to the north by the rocky promontory of Filey Brigg, was popular by the beginning of the C19 with visitors escaping from crowded Scarborough. By 1828 its amenities included a spa well, bathing machines, fishing boats for hire, and a free library. An enterprising Birmingham solicitor, John Wilkes Unett, bought thirty-five acres south of the village in 1835 and had plans prepared for hotels and elegant houses including a grand crescent. The Crescent was completed by the late 1850s and contributed to Filey's image as a genteel resort which attracted affluent visitors. The heyday of Filey was just before the First World War. It has now become residential, with its economy dependent largely on day visitors. Nevertheless, unlike the East Riding's other seaside towns, Filey has neither decayed nor become totally commercialized.

The Crescent, Filey

Following London fashion, these dignified lodgings for respectable summer visitors are stuccoed to look like stone, and have a minimum of classical ornament. Decoration is provided by elegant iron balconies, which help to emphasise the position of the chief reception rooms on the first floor. By dividing up The Crescent, it is possible to give the houses at the ends of each block an outlook in more than one direction. The earliest C18 seaside resorts had avoided building on bracing sites overlooking the sea, but by the end of the century Brighton was setting the pattern for grand crescents and terraces with sea views. The taste for formal neo-classical planning, fuelled by the popularity of Grand Tours to the Mediterranean, became widespread during the early C19. The use of the austere Greek Doric order for porch columns, although highly fashionable around 1820, was on the way out by the time Filey was being developed, and appears only on the earlier buildings.

David Neave

ABOVE: A pair of Greek Doric porches at the south elevation of the earliest section of The Crescent, Filey, built 1840–1. The cast-iron balcony has an anthemion motif.

RIGHT: Late Victorian arcade of shops, Quay Road, Bridlington.

BELOW: The Crescent, Filey. The Royal Crescent Hotel (now Royal Crescent Court, second from left, was designed by John Petch of Scarborough and built in 1853. Its nine bays and four storeys make it the most prestigious building in The Crescent, with a large portico on paired Doric columns, and a balustrade fronting a Venetian window above. Second from the right is the first part of the Crescent to be built, designed by John Petch of Scarborough 1840–1.

Bridlington

Bridlington is two towns: the Old Town to the north, and the Quay with its harbour and seafront, which emerged as a genteel bathing resort in the mid-C18 and was transformed with the opening of the railway line from Hull in 1846. Large hotels and extensive stuccoed terraces were built dominating the seafront. Unlike Filey, Bridlington continued to develop in the C20, with the large Expanse Hotel of 1937 and the Spa Royal Hall and Theatre built in 1932. Both are in a variation of the International Modern style with bows and balconies. The most distinctive of the inter-war seaside housing, along South Marine Drive and streets off, is a series of Swiss-style timber chalets and on Belvedere Parade a trio of modest rendered villas.

David Neave

Eddie Ryle-Hodges

David Neave

Early C20 Swiss chalet style houses on South Cliff, Bridlington.

David Neave

Inter-war seaside villas, Belvedere Parade, Bridlington.

Expanse Hotel, North Marine Drive, Bridlington. Built in 1937 to the designs of E.C. Briggs.

Questions to consider

■ How has the location of houses near the seashore influenced their design?

■ How has the development of the resorts balanced the needs of residents and holiday makers?

■ What impact have different forms of transport had on architecture in the coastal resorts?

an extensive development of large detached houses along tree-lined boulevards and a pier at the end of Young Street. It came to nothing and in 1873 a local newspaper reported that the town was 'still in a dormant state, and plans which looked so elaborate on paper seem to have vanished into thin air'. A pier was built in 1877 opposite the railway station, but following repeated damage by storms it was dismantled c.1900. A brief period of popularity for the resort in Edwardian times was followed by stagnation until recent years when much new housing has been built.

Withernsea

Withernsea is an interesting example of how investors and architects cannot by themselves motivate people to live or holiday on a stretch of the coast lacking the scenic quality of the East Riding's northern section. The Hull and Holderness Railway Company believed the twin settlements of Withernsea and Owthorne (combined population 272) were ripe for development in 1854 when its railway line opened from Hull. The railway company immediately built the forty-bedroomed Queen's Hotel with pleasure grounds beside the station and commissioned the same architect, Cuthbert Brodrick, to plan broad streets with elegant terraces on twenty-one acres of land north of the station. Bannister and Young Streets were laid out but only Nos. 57–59 Bannister Street were built in the 1850s and then not to Brodrick's design. In 1871 the Withernsea Pier, Promenade, Gas and General Improvement Co. Ltd proposed another ambitious scheme for

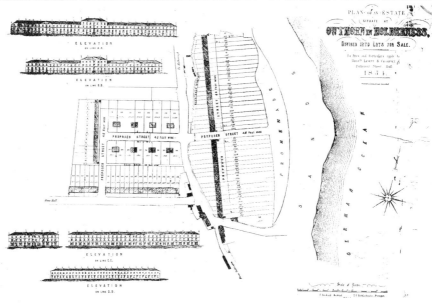

ABOVE RIGHT: Queen's Hotel, Withernsea by Cuthbert Brodrick. Built 1854–5 at cost of £10,530. The anticipated crowds of visitors did not come and the hotel proved too large and too costly. It became a convalescent home in 1892. The ruined church of St Nicholas, Withernsea, can be seen on the left and Withernsea railway station on the right.
BELOW RIGHT: Cuthbert Brodrick's ambitious plans of 1854.

THE PORT OF HULL

By the C19 Hull ranked third amongst Britain's ports. Trade in wool and then cloth laid the foundations of the port in the Middle Ages along with its role as an English base for campaigns against the Scots. In 1293 Edward I acquired the small wool-exporting port of Wyke on the River Hull from the Abbey of Meaux and renamed it Kingston-upon-Hull. A sizeable town was planned and in 1321 Edward II licensed the building of a ditch and crenellated wall around the town. The only visible remains of Hull's walls, the most extensive brick structure in medieval England, are the foundations of Beverley Gate and some adjoining wall at the west end of Whitefriargate.

Merchants' Houses

Medieval merchants built their houses and warehouses on the High Street which curves along the west side of the River Hull. Trade with the Netherlands, important from the Middle Ages, expanded in the C17 and had a marked influence on both the design and materials of Hull's buildings. The wealthy merchants rebuilt their timber-framed buildings in brick, using Dutch pantiles for the roofs, small Dutch bricks for floors and courtyards and Delft tile surrounds for their fireplaces. Fashion dictated a change in style in the C18 when some merchants were again rebuilding their homes along the High Street. Maister House (National Trust), rebuilt after a fire in 1744, is the finest. Other C18 merchants' houses include Nos. 23–24 High Street and Blaydes House, No. 6 High Street. Later in the C18 merchants escaped in the summer months from the noise and smells of the port to their country villas to the west of town or moved to one of the elegant new terraces being erected in the northern suburb (see pp.28–9).

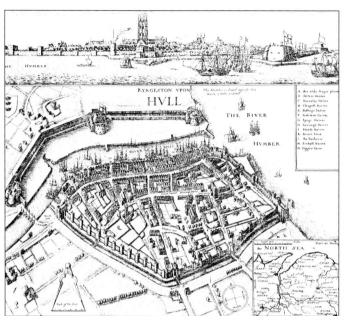

LEFT: Wenceslas Hollar's bird's-eye view of 1640 shows the walled town looking east. The dense development along the River Hull is clearly visible. The almost empty site in the foreground (above the flag), is the site of the Carmelite Friary later developed for Trinity House, a merchants' guild, which became the chief authority for shipping and navigation in the C17 and C18.

RIGHT: By the C18 elaborate surface ornament of the kind used at Wilberforce House had gone out of fashion for exteriors. Maister House was built in 1744–5 by the Hull architect Joseph Page with advice from Lord Burlington. It is plain outside, but inside there is a magnificent top-lit stone staircase with an ornate wrought iron balustrade. It rises around a square hall to the first floor, to provide a grand approach to the main reception rooms. Walls and underside of the stairs are sumptuously decorated with plasterwork.

RCHME

A.F.Kersting

University of Hull

ABOVE: Artisan Mannerist detail on porch of Wilberforce House.

ABOVE: Wilberforce House, now a museum, set between the High Street and the river, was probably built in the 1660s by the bricklayer William Catlyn, Hull's leading artisan–architect of the later C17. Its elaborate decoration reflects the influence of the ornate classical style developed in the Netherlands. Both the brick walls and the Corinthian pilasters to the upper storey are rusticated, with stone 'jewels' used to decorate the pilasters and the aprons below the windows. The gatepiers are contemporary. Sash windows and the plain parapet date from an C18 remodelling for the Wilberforce family.

Docks and Warehouses

Until the later C18 all shipping loaded and unloaded along the River Hull. The merchants' staithes and a handful of warehouses survive on the west side of the river. With the growth of whale fishing, increasing congestion led to the construction of the first purpose-built dock in 1778, later known as the Queen's Dock. This involved destruction of the medieval walls on the north side of the town. Further docks followed around the western edge of the Old Town and along the line of the former town walls. From the later C19 these early docks were superseded by those which were developed along the Humber and which are still in use.

Warehouses on the west side of the River Hull. The four-storey range on the left was built for Joseph Pease in 1745 and 1760.

LEFT: The Humber Dock. Built 1809, used as a marina from 1983.

Using older maps it is still possible to trace the development of the port, despite many C20 changes in the town centre. A wide range of warehouses survive, especially on the west bank of the River Hull. Many have been converted to other uses, among them the C18 Pease warehouses, now flats (best seen from Drypool Bridge), two mid–late C19 warehouses on Guildhall Road, one now offices, the other a library, and three C19 warehouses near Princes Dock, which have become the Waterfront Hotel.

The first Dock Offices of 1820 were succeeded in 1867–71 by much grander Offices at the west end of Queen's Dock, an impressive building in a Venetian Renaissance style cleverly contrived by C.G. Wray on an awkward triangular site. Maritime themes dominate the decoration. Appropriately, the building is now the Town Docks Museum housing the city's maritime collection.

The Dock Offices of 1867–71 by C.G. Wray.

Questions to consider

■ Which are the chief features of the historic port that are recognisable today?

■ How have the city authorities commemorated the port's history? Are there other ways in which it could be commemorated?

■ What should be done with redundant docks and warehouses? Do recent conversions maintain the character of the original buildings?

■ The merchants' houses illustrate changing taste in the use of classical decoration. Compare how ornament is used on different buildings.

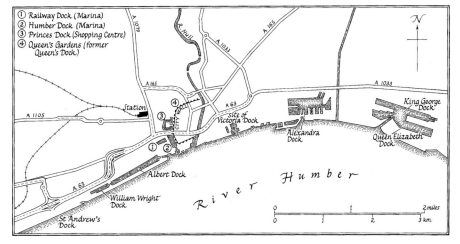

① Railway Dock (Marina)
② Humber Dock (Marina)
③ Princes Dock (Shopping Centre)
④ Queen's Gardens (former Queen's Dock)

Hull Docks

Dock	Opened	Present use
Queen's Dock	1778	Filled in (1930), now Queen's Gardens. Entrance now a dry dock
Humber Dock	1809	Marina since 1983
Princes Dock	1829	Shopping Centre built 1987–90
Railway Dock	1846	Part of Marina since 1983
East Hull: Victoria Dock	1850	Filled in (late 1970s), housing built
Alexandra Dock	1885	Still in use
King George Dock	1914	Still in use
Queen Elizabeth Dock	1969	Still in use
West Hull: Albert Dock	1869	Still in use
William Wright Dock	1880	Still in use
St Andrew's Dock	1883	Partly filled in (late 1980s)

ARCHITECTURAL STYLES IN HULL 1830–1930

Hull's principal buildings reflect its prosperity throughout the Victorian period and its enhanced status when made a city in 1897. The great range of architectural styles favoured in the latter part of the C19 and early C20 are well-represented. Architects were much concerned with the problem of finding appropriate styles for the varied building types which developed during this period of rapid expansion and change. They drew on both the Gothic and classical traditions to convey suitable images, but had to adapt these styles to fit the needs of the times. Large buildings, made possible by the use of iron construction, set new challenges. Prefabricated detail, such as terracotta ornament, provided new opportunities for relatively inexpensive decoration. The commissions, sometimes won in public competition, went to both provincial and more celebrated London-based architects.

BM Photographic Services

Bill Marsden

LEFT: Hymers College. Gothic, with its religious overtones, was often considered appropriately serious for educational buildings in the mid C19, but in the 1890s architects did not hesitate to mix styles to produce picturesque results. Here Jacobean gables and classical entrance are combined with Gothic windows.

BELOW: Punch Hotel. Buildings for entertainment inspired greater frivolity. This late Gothic and Jacobean extravaganza faintly reminiscent of Renaissance France, advertises itself by fanciful gables, pierced tracery and lively lettering. Much of the detail is of terracotta, with glazed panels of Burmantofts Faience.

ABOVE: Guildhall. The pride and grandeur of Edwardian Hull is expressed by an immense array of giant composite columns between central and end pavilions crowned by colossal groups of sculpture (Maritime Prowess at one end, Strength, symbolised by Britannia, at the other). The entrance wing with clock tower is an addition of 1913–16, which replaced Brodrick's town hall of 1862.

BM Photographic Services

Questions to consider

■ How well do the buildings' exterior designs suit their purpose? What impression were they intended to make on the visitor?

■ Where buildings are open to the public, investigate how they are planned inside. How well did they serve those who worked in them?

■ Compare the ways in which classical detail has been used for Hull's public buildings. Which compositions do you find most successful?

■ Look at the ways in which sculpture can be used on buildings. Which examples do you find most effective, and why?

■ How do other schools and pubs in Hull compare with those illustrated here?

RIGHT: City Hall. Joseph Hirst was Hull's first City Architect. He designed this concert hall and art gallery with its two-tier portico and dome in the free Baroque style that was so often adopted for Edwardian public buildings.

ABOVE: Former College of Art. Here classical features are used freely in an effectively flamboyant manner. Red brick is contrasted with striking stone quoins and bands. Above the recessed centre the deep eaves of the pedimental gable shelter a mosaic portraying the arts, executed by the Bromsgrove Guild.

Tower Cinema. The ornate classical façade of green and cream faience includes some entertaining Art Nouveau details. An allegorical female figure sits on the parapet and above the rounded corners are two domes decorated with green and yellow mosaic.

Ferens Art Gallery. Classicism continued popular for public buildings between the wars, although it was generally expressed in a quieter and more restrained form. The recessed entrance is dignified by Corinthian columns.

Architectural styles of a sample of Hull's buildings

Building	Style	Date	Architect
Paragon Railway Station	Italianate	1846–8	G.T. Andrews of York
The Exchange (now Juvenile and Domestic Courts) Lowgate	Italianate	1865–6	W. Botterill of Hull
Dock Offices (now Town Docks Museum) Queen Victoria Square	Venetian Renaissance	1867–71	C.G. Wray of London
General Post Office (now The Old Custom House) Market Place	Italianate	1877	J. Williams of London
Charterhouse Lane School	Gothic	1881	W. Botterill of Hull
Newington Primary School Dairycoates Ave	Queen Anne	1885	J. Bilson of Hull
Hymers College Hymers Avenue	Jacobean	1893	J. Bilson of Hull
Northern Library Beverley Road	Gothic	1895	Cheers of London
Punch Hotel	Gothic and Jacobean	1896	Smith, Brodrick & Lowther of Hull
Central Library Albion Street	Edwardian Baroque	1900–1	J.S. Gibson of London
City Hall Queen Victoria Square	Edwardian Baroque	1903–9	J.H. Hirst of Hull
Former College of Art Anlaby Road	Free Classical	1904	E.A. Rickards of London
Guildhall Alfred Gelder Street	Neo-classical	1904–16	E. Cooper of London
General Post Office Lowgate	Edwardian Imperial	1908–9	W. Potts of London
Tower Cinema Anlaby Road	Classical with Art Noveau details	1914	H.P. Binks of Hull
Ferens Art Gallery Queen Victoria Square	Classical	1924–7	S.N. Cooke & E.C. Davies of London

HOUSING IN HULL: VICTORIAN TO MODERN

Hull's population grew rapidly in the C19 and early C20, rising from 32,958 in 1831 to a peak of around 321,500 in 1936. How was this increasing population housed? Until the later C18 Hull's population was confined within the medieval town walls; only with the demolition of the walls for the building of the docks between 1778 and 1829 did the town begin to expand.

Victorian middle-class housing

The merchants were the first to leave the Old Town, abandoning their houses on the High Street for a country residence in one of the villages to the west of Hull – Cottingham, Kirk Ella, Hessle, North Ferriby or Welton, or a fashionable terraced house in the new northern suburb. By the mid-Victorian period Hull's growing middle classes were seeking homes segregated from their workforce. They were provided for first at Pearson Park, laid out in 1860–2 on open country to the west of Beverley Road. A shipowner and merchant, Zachariah Pearson, then Mayor of Hull, presented the town with a twenty-seven-acre site for a public park, retaining ten acres around three sides for sites for 'villa residences'. Grand detached houses were rapidly built in a variety of Italianate and Gothic styles. Immediately to the west of Pearson Park are 'The Avenues', laid out for David P. Garbutt, shipowner and

shipbuilder, in 1874–5, as a series of tree-lined boulevards running east to west. At the same period, William Botterill was laying out Newland Park to the south of Cottingham Road with surprising originality, with curving streets, large gardens and plenty of trees – an early garden suburb. Development here was slow, and after thirty years only 15 out of 90 plots had been built on.

Court housing

The working population at first continued to cram into the Old Town, taking over the merchants' mansions as tenements and lining the yards and former gardens with cottages. In the early C19 these close-built yards with tunnel entrances provided the model for the new housing being built to the west of the Old Town in Myton.

University of Hull

Improved as a result of byelaws passed from 1854 onwards, cul-de-sac court housing, distinctive to Hull, continued to be built up to the First World War. Many examples can still be seen, for example off Newland Avenue and Holderness Road.

Model dwellings

One unusual attempt to improve the standard of mid-Victorian working class housing is Turner Court, built as model dwellings for 32 families by the Society for Improving the Condition of the Labouring Classes in 1862, its only project outside London. The large two-storey building is arranged around a courtyard. Accommodation was provided in five one-bedroomed, nineteen two-bedroomed and eight three-bedroomed flats.

ABOVE LEFT: Cul-de-sac court, Princes Road. Built in the 1880s. The courts, some twenty feet in width, a minimum distance determined by byelaws, ran at right angles to the main road, with six to ten houses on each side. At the end a wall or fence usually divided one court from the next which led off a parallel street.

ABOVE RIGHT: Turner Court, Midland Street, designed by Henry M. Eyton in 1862, has been modernised but the exterior is unaltered. The variety of materials, white brick with red brick and stone dressings, suggests concern to provide a building that was attractive as well as useful.

BM Photographic Services

Amongst the first houses west of Pearson Park were eight designed by George Gilbert Scott junior in 1877–9 for his cousin, John Cooper, a Hull solicitor. The relationship explains the unusual employment of a London architect in the Hull suburb. The houses, on the west side of Salisbury Street and round the corner into Park and Westbourne Avenues, are in the latest fashion, the so-called 'Queen Anne' style pioneered in the 1870s by Norman Shaw. Picturesque shaped gables and red brickwork are used to create friendly domestic architecture inspired by C17 precedent, in reaction to the formal classical or spiky Gothic of mid-Victorian years.

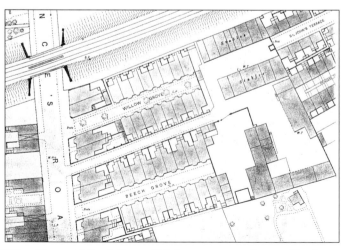

Willow Grove and Beech Grove. Cul-de-sac courts on the east side of Princes Road (Ordnance Survey plan 1892).

Hull Garden Village in 1928. The tree-lined avenues flanked by semi-detached or short blocks of houses set in large gardens contrast with the contemporary close-built terraces and cul-de-sac courts of the adjoining roads.

Hull Garden Village

A more ambitious venture was undertaken in the early C20 by the Hull starch manufacturer, Sir James Reckitt. Following the example of fellow Quaker industrialists such as George Cadbury at Bournville and Joseph Rowntree at New Earswick, he wished to improve the housing of his workforce.

'It seems to me the time has come ... to establish a Garden Village, within a reasonable distance of our Works, so that those who are wishful might have the opportunity of living in a better house, with a garden, for the same rent that they now pay for a house in Hull – with the advantages of fresher air, and such Clubs, and out-door amusements, as are usually found in rural surroundings.'
(James Reckitt, 1907.)

Land was bought on the north side of Holderness Road and by 1913 over 500 houses had been completed to the designs of the local architects Runton and Barry. Five grades of houses were built at twelve to the acre, all with gardens. They have walls of roughcast brickwork, corner buttresses, tile-hung or half-timbered gables and wide-eaved roofs which sweep low to encompass porches. Central amenities were provided at the Oval, a large green with the village hall and the club house. A shopping centre in late C17 style is arranged around three sides of a courtyard with colonnaded shops on the ground floor. There are three sets of half-timbered almshouses for the retired workers on the edge of the 'village'.

Council Housing

Not far from the Garden Village is Hull's earliest surviving local authority housing to the south of Holderness Road on Rustenburg Street, Steynburg Street and Newbridge Road. The brick terraced or semi-detached houses with canted bay windows and rendering to the first floor, were built in 1902–3 for families displaced when slum housing was cleared for the building of Alfred Gelder Street to the south of the Guildhall. Slum clearance led to extensive council house building in the inter-war period, both on the edge of the city and on cleared sites. The destruction caused by bombing in the Second World War and post-war clearances accelerated such developments. Between 1945 and 1989 council-built homes in Hull rose from c.10,500 to over 50,000, accounting for almost fifty per cent of the city's housing stock.

Questions to consider

■ Compare the advantages and disadvantages of living in the city and in a suburb. How have conditions changed since the C19?

■ Compare the architectural styles for housing developments in different areas and for different types of people. What can they tell you about the attitudes and intentions of those who planned them?

■ How does the Garden Village compare with its rural equivalent, the estate village? (See pp.14–15.)

■ How could the planners improve the appearance of a large council housing estate within the inevitable budget constraints?

■ What amenities would be desirable in any housing development?

Hull Garden Village, semi-detached houses, Beech Avenue. This is a third grade house with sitting room, kitchen, with bath and three or four bedrooms. The windows have been modernized.

The Porter Street flats, designed by David Harvey, the City Architect, in 1938. A good example of a civic housing scheme. The five-storey brick building with balconies and rounded staircase towers surrounds an open landscaped courtyard. Decoration is kept to a minimum, with just a little brick banding.

MODERN ARCHITECTURE

In the Middle Ages and early modern period, the major buildings in the East Riding were erected by the great landowners and the church. During the late C18 and C19 much of the building work in rural areas was still financed by the landed gentry but in the towns commercial and trading interests, along with the municipal authorities, were responsible for the most imposing buildings. Who has commissioned new buildings in the second half of the C20?

Major buildings in the previous two centuries have looked to various forms of classical or medieval architecture for inspiration. From the 1930s modernism rejected the stylistic trappings of these traditions as irrelevant, and concentrated on responding to the functions of buildings, relying on good proportions and materials rather than decoration for aesthetic appeal. What principles have been adopted for the design of buildings of the late C20?

When any new building is planned it has to take its place with existing buildings. There could, for example, be restrictions on the height of a building so that it conforms to the established roof line. There may be recommendations by the planning authority about the use of materials or detail sympathetic to neighbouring buildings. To what extent have recent buildings fitted in with their surroundings? Is this a desirable aim?

For many centuries, the East Riding's buildings depended on local resources for their building materials. What impact have newer materials, such as concrete and steel, had on buildings' appearance and design? To examine these questions, four categories of buildings will be considered: housing, education, public and commercial buildings, and industry and communications.

Housing
Private housing in the East Riding from the 1950s–70s was usually on the edge of existing settlements and rarely paid much regard to design or context. From the 1980s deliberate efforts were made in both Hull and Beverley to provide housing on inner town sites, and greater concern was shown by planners to integrate new building with the historic environment.

Education
Some of the more adventurous recent buildings have been built for educational use. The earliest buildings on the campus of the University of Hull on Cottingham Road, begun in 1928, are of dark-red brick in a Neo-Georgian style. The 1960s buildings abandoned traditional styles. The most prominent is the eight-storey library block. The most original, although controversial, recent school building in the region is the Perronet Thompson

British Steel

Perronet Thompson School, Bransholme, Hull, 1987 by the Humberside County Architect.

School at Bransholme, Hull. This futuristic design of 1987 by the Humberside County Architect has a steel frame clad in buff-coloured concrete blocks. The central spine comprising sports hall, gymnasium and library is covered by an 80 metres long glazed barrel-vault. On either side are three linked blocks of classrooms with sloping silvered roofs. It forms a deliberate and striking contrast to the surrounding housing.

RCHME

Eastgate, Beverley. This site close to Beverley Minster, once occupied by a Palladian mansion and later by industry, was developed with superior private housing in the late 1980s and early 1990s. In reaction to the simplicity of the modern tradition, a variety of materials is used – brown brick with light brown and blue brick bands, with decorative stone details and timber and lead-covered bays. The houses are grouped around courtyards and include a sheltered housing complex bounded by the restored medieval friary.

James Austin

The Lawns, Cottingham, is a series of students' residences for the University of Hull of 1963–6 by Gillespie, Kidd and Coia. The simple cubic forms of the individual brick blocks are clustered together on a staggered plan; from a distance they give the impression of a long undulating wall set in a picturesque landscape.

Hull Crown Courts by Building Design Partnership, 1988-90.

Princes Quay Shopping Centre, Hull, by Hugh Martin Partnership, 1988-91.

Public and commercial buildings

On the edge of the Old Town of Hull, linked by Alfred Gelder Street, two prominent buildings of the late 1980s have also produced mixed reactions. The Hull Crown Court, built in 1988–90, with its silvered domes, and the classical references incorporated in its brick façade, echoes the details of the Town Docks Museum and the City Hall as well as the nearby Guildhall and the General Post Office. Less compromising is the Princes Quay Shopping Centre which fills much of the former Princes Dock. The massive metallic marquee which dominates the heart of the city is partly built on stilts over the water. Posts and cables holding up the roof suggest the masts and rigging of sailing ships.

Industry and communications

Civil engineers, working with architects, have produced some of the region's most memorable modern structures. Coal mining came to the East Riding in the 1980s with the development of four mines for the Selby coalfield at Deighton, Riccall, Skipwith and Stillingfleet. It was a challenge to make the pit-head buildings of drum winder-house, fan house and shaft towers harmonise with the rural setting. This has been achieved by constructing low-profiled buildings clad in red brick or cream blockwork and skilful landscaping.

The most magnificent modern structure is without doubt the Humber Bridge, the world's longest single span suspension bridge when built between 1972 and 1981, by the engineers Freeman, Fox & Partners. Its massive tapering concrete towers support the cables from which the roadway is suspended. For many visitors to the East Riding it will be the first and last building of the area which they see.

RIGHT: Stillingfleet mine, pit-head buildings by Fletcher, Ross & Hickling, completed 1984.

BELOW: The Humber Bridge, 1972-81, by Freeman Fox & Partners seen from the north, towering over Whiting Mill built in 1810 for crushing chalkstone from a nearby quarry.

GLOSSARY

APRON: raised panel below a window or wall monument or tablet.

ARCADE: series of arches supported by piers or columns. Blind arcade or arcading: the same applied to the wall surface.

ASHLAR: masonry of large blocks wrought to even faces and square edges.

BARGEBOARDS: boards often carved or fretted, fixed beneath the eaves of a gable to cover and protect the rafters.

BASILICA: a Roman public hall; hence an aisled building with a clerestory.

BAY: division of an elevation or interior space as defined by regular vertical features such as arches, columns, windows etc.

BAY WINDOW: window of one or more storeys projecting from the face of a building. Canted: with a straight front and angled sides. Bow-window: curved. Oriel: rests on corbels or brackets and starts above ground level; also the bay window at the dais end of a medieval great hall.

BOND: the pattern of long sides (stretchers) and short ends (headers) produced on the face of a wall by laying bricks in a particular way. See fig. 1.

CAPITAL: head or crowning feature of a column or pilaster. See figs. 2, 4.

CLASSICAL: inspired by the traditions of Ancient Greece and Rome, particularly the use of the ORDERS (q.v.). See figs. 4, 5.

COADE STONE: ceramic artificial stone made in Lambeth 1769 – c. 1840 by Eleanor Coade (†1821) and her associates.

COFFERING: arrangement of sunken panels (coffers), square or polygonal, decorating a ceiling, vault or arch.

COLONNADE: range of columns supporting an entablature. Cf. Arcade.

COLUMN: a classical, upright structural member of round section with a shaft, a capital, and

usually a base. See fig. 4.

CROCKETS: leafy hooks. Crocketing decorates the edges of Gothic features, such as pinnacles, canopies etc. See fig. 2.

CUPOLA: small dome on a circular or polygonal base crowning a larger dome, roof or turret.

MOULDING: shaped ornamental strip of continuous section. See fig. 2.

MULLION: vertical member between window lights. See fig. 3.

ORDER: one of a series of recessed arches and jambs forming a splayed medieval opening, e.g. a doorway or arcade arch. See fig. 2.

ORDERS: the formalized versions of the post-and-lintel system in classical architecture. The main orders are Doric, Ionic and Corinthian. They are Greek in origin but occur in Roman versions. Tuscan is a simple version of Roman Doric. Though each order has its own conventions, there are many minor variations. The Composite capital combines Ionic volutes with Corinthian foliage. Superimposed orders: orders on successive levels, usually in the upward sequence of Tuscan, Doric, Ionic, Corinthian, Composite. Giant Order: order whose height is that of two or more storeys of the building to which it is applied. See fig. 4.

PILASTER: flat representation of a classical column in shallow relief.

ROTUNDA: building or room circular in plan.

RUSTICATION: Exaggerated treatment of masonry to give an effect of strength. See fig. 1.

QUOINS: dressed stones at the angles of a building. See fig. 1.

SCAGLIOLA: composition imitating marble.

SHAFT: vertical member of round or polygonal section. Shaft-ring: at the junction of shafts set *en delit* or attached to a pier or wall. See fig. 2, 4.

STUCCO: fine lime plaster worked to a smooth surface.

TRACERY: openwork pattern of masonry or timber in upper part of an opening. Blind tracery: applied to a solid wall. Plate tracery, introduced c. 1200: in which shapes are cut through solid masonry. Bar tracery, introduced into England c. 1250: intersecting moulded ribwork continued from the mullions, especially elaborate during the Decorated period. Types of tracery include geometric: c. 1250–1310; Y-tracery: c. 1300; intersecting: c. 1300; reticulated: early C14; curvilinear: C14; panel: mid C14–early C16. See fig. 2.

TRANSOM: horizontal member separating window lights. See fig. 3.

VAULT: arched stone roof. Tunnel vault: continuous semicircular or pointed arch, often of rubble masonry. Rib vault: with masonry framework of intersecting arches.

MEDIEVAL STYLES: See fig. 2.

ANGLO-SAXON: English architecture from before the Norman Conquest of 1066.

ROMANESQUE: current in the C11 and C12. In England often called Norman. Characterised by the use of semicircular arches, sometimes with elaborate mouldings.

TRANSITIONAL: generally used for the phase between Romanesque and Early English (c. 1175 – c. 1200).

GOTHIC: current from the late C12 to the early C16, in England generally subdivided by its tracery types (q.v.):

E.E. (EARLY ENGLISH): c. 1190–1250, characterised by pointed arches, lancet windows and plate tracery;

DEC (DECORATED): c. 1290 to c. 1350, so named after its elaborate window types;

PERP (PERPENDICULAR): c. 1335–50 to c. 1530, referring to its use of upright tracery panels.

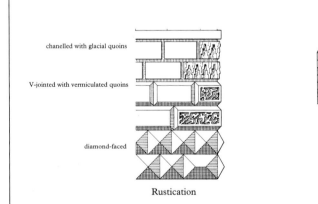

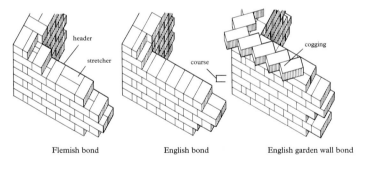

Rustication

Brickwork

Flemish bond   English bond   English garden wall bond

chanelled with glacial quoins

V-jointed with vermiculated quoins

diamond-faced

header

stretcher

course

cogging

Fig. 1 Building techniques

Some commonly used stylistic terms

1000	1100	1200	1300	1400	1500

ANGLO-SAXON.......

TUDOR..................

Elizabeth

NORMAN/ROMANESQUE................

RENAISSANC
/CLASSICA

GOTHIC..........

Early English .....Geometric......Decorated............

Perpendicular..

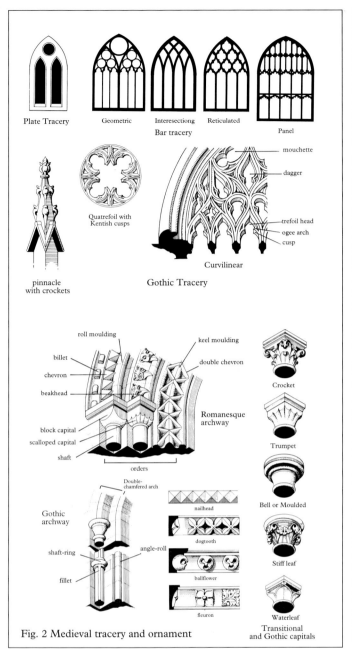

Plate Tracery

Geometric

Interesectiong

Reticulated

Panel

Bar tracery

Quatrefoil with Kentish cusps

mouchette

dagger

trefoil head

ogee arch

cusp

Curvilinear

pinnacle with crockets

Gothic Tracery

roll moulding

keel moulding

billet

double chevron

chevron

beakhead

block capital

scalloped capital

shaft

Romanesque archway

orders

Crocket

Trumpet

Bell or Moulded

Stiff leaf

Waterleaf

Gothic archway

Double-chamfered arch

shaft-ring

angle-roll

fillet

nailhead

dogtooth

ballflower

fleuron

Transitional and Gothic capitals

Fig. 2 Medieval tracery and ornament

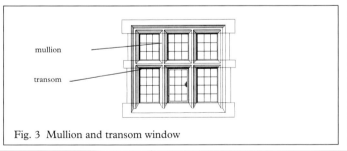

mullion

transom

Fig. 3 Mullion and transom window

Entablature

Column

Shaft

Drum

Abacus

Capital

Arris

Flute

Greek Doric

tympanum

Portico

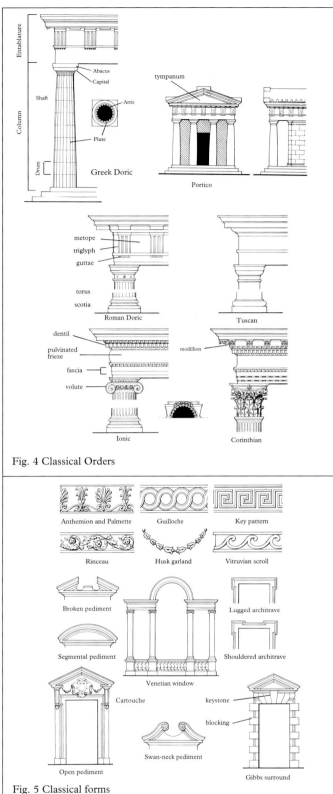

metope

triglyph

guttae

torus

scotia

Roman Doric

Tuscan

dentil

pulvinated frieze

fascia

volute

modillion

Ionic

Corinthian

Fig. 4 Classical Orders

Anthemion and Palmette

Guilloche

Key pattern

Rinceau

Husk garland

Vitruvian scroll

Broken pediment

Lugged architrave

Segmental pediment

Shouldered architrave

Venetian window

Cartouche

keystone

blocking

Open pediment

Swan-neck pediment

Gibbs surround

Fig. 5 Classical forms

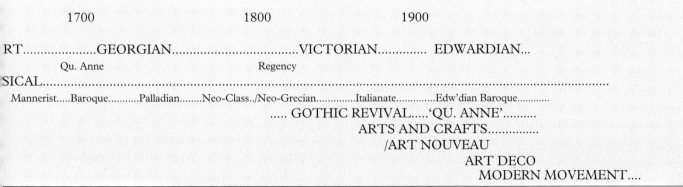

1700	1800	1900

RT.................GEORGIAN................................VICTORIAN............. EDWARDIAN...

Qu. Anne

Regency

SICAL...

Mannerist.....Baroque...........Palladian.......Neo-Class../Neo-Grecian.............Italianate.............Edw'dian Baroque...........

..... GOTHIC REVIVAL.....'QU. ANNE'..........

ARTS AND CRAFTS..............

/ART NOUVEAU

ART DECO

MODERN MOVEMENT....

33

Printed and archive sources:

Local history libraries at Hull, York, Beverley and Bridlington and York Minster Library have comprehensive collections on the region. Older books are listed in A.G. Dickens and K.A. MacMahon, *A guide to regional studies on the East Riding of Yorkshire and the City of Hull* (1956). The more up-to-date *East Yorkshire Bibliography*, a Hull University Library computer database, is accessible at the University Library and Hull and Beverley local history libraries and nationally through most academic libraries or via a modem. B. Dyson (ed.), *A Guide to Local Studies in East Yorkshire* (1985) provides useful information on printed and documentary sources. See also Further Reading in N. Pevsner and D. Neave, *Buildings of England: Yorkshire: York and the East Riding* (1995). The local history libraries also have excellent collections of illustrations – prints, old postcards and more recent photographs, and other original primary sources including early Ordnance Survey Plans, local newspapers, e.g. *York Courant, Hull Advertiser, Beverley Guardian* and *Bridlington Free Press*, and trade directories from the late C18.

There are the four **regional archive offices**. **Humberside County Archive Office**, County Hall, Champney Road, Beverley, has official records of present and former local authorities also covering schools, police stations, workhouses and byelaw plans from the mid C19; document collections from solicitors and some large estate collections (including Burton Constable); C16–C20 maps and plans; parish records for the Archdeaconry of the East Riding (eastern two-thirds of the riding) including much on church building and furnishings and Nonconformist records; the Deeds Registry for the East Riding and Hull.

Borthwick Institute of Historical Research, University of York, St Anthony's Hall, Peasholme Green, York, is the York Diocesan record office; it contains records of church buildings, furnishings and fittings (faculty applications from C18–C20); parsonage houses; deposited parish records for the Archdeaconry of York (western third of East Riding). See C.C. Webb, 'Sources for the History of Houses at the Borthwick Institute' in *Borthwick Institute Bulletin* 3 (1986).

University Archives, Brynmor Jones Library, University of Hull, Cottingham Road, Hull, has archives of East Riding landed estates, e.g. the Sykes family of Sledmere, Hothams of South Dalton and Wenlocks of Escrick, much on country houses and other estate buildings (plans, building accounts, correspondence); original maps and plans. See B. Dyson,

Yorkshire Maps and Plans in the Archives of the University of Hull (1990). **Hull City Record Office**, 79 Lowgate, Hull, has official records of the corporation; material on C19 and C20 public buildings and byelaw plans from the mid C19; some records of architectural firms.

Museums and Art Galleries:

These are a good source of illustrative material and artefacts relevant to the study of local buildings. The Ferens Art Gallery, Hull, has the most extensive collection of paintings, prints and drawings. Other important holdings are at York City Art Gallery, York Minster Library, Beverley Art Gallery, and Sewerby Hall and The Bayle, Bridlington. The latter two have displays of period interiors as does Hornsea Museum, the Wilberforce House Museum, High Street, Hull, and the Castle Museum, York. The history and development of Hull is covered in the Old Grammar School Museum, South Church Side, Hull, and the history of the port of Hull at the Town Docks Museum, Queen Victoria Square. Archaeological material is well displayed at the Hull and East Riding Museum (High Street, Hull), Yorkshire Museum (Museum Gardens, York) and at Malton Museum. Agriculture and transport are dealt with at the Yorkshire Museum of Farming, Murton, York, and the Streetlife Museum, High Street, Hull. The re-erected buildings at Ryedale Folk Museum, Hutton-le-Hole, North Yorkshire, are relevant to the study of local traditional buildings.

Buildings open to the public:

Most of the museums and art galleries listed above are located in buildings of architectural interest. A great range of other buildings are accessible. With some perseverance access can be gained to almost all Anglican churches: those open each day include Beverley Minster, St Mary, Beverley, Holy Trinity, Hull (times advertised), Bridlington Priory, St Patrick, Patrington, St Peter, Howden and St Michael, Garton-on-the-Wolds. Burton Agnes Hall, Burton Constable Hall and Sledmere House are country houses open in the summer months. Burton Agnes Manor House, Skipsea Castle, Kirkham Priory and Wharram Percy deserted medieval village are English Heritage sites. The magnificent staircase hall of Maister House, High Street, Hull (National Trust), can be visited on weekdays.

General works on the East Riding:

The basic reference work is the *Victoria County History: East Riding*; six volumes, out of a projected ten, have been published covering the towns of Hull (vol. 1, 1969) and

Beverley (vol. 6, 1989) as well as some 80 towns and villages. Useful earlier regional topographical works are the two volumes on Holderness by George Poulson, 1840–1, J.J. Sheahan and T. Whellan, *History and Topography of the City of York and the East Riding of Yorkshire*, two volumes 1855–6, and T. Bulmer, *History, Topography & Directory of East Yorkshire* (1892, reprinted 1985). General histories of the East Riding are provided by the early C20 school text books by H.B. Browne (1912) and J.L. Brockbank (1913). Many historical topics have been covered on a regional basis in the admirable series of booklets published by the East Yorkshire Local History Society since 1951. *Humber Perspectives* (1990), edited by S. Ellis and D.R. Crowther, has valuable short essays on the archaeology, historical geography, and urban development of the wider region. N. Pevsner and D. Neave, *Buildings of England: Yorkshire: York and the East Riding* (1995) is a comprehensive guide with a detailed introduction providing an overview of the architectural history of the region with much information on architects and craftsmen. The principal local periodicals for history, archaeology, and architectural history are the *Yorkshire Archaeological Journal*, the *Transactions of the East Riding Antiquarian Society* and the *Transactions of the Georgian Society for East Yorkshire* (1938–63). Detailed architectural descriptions in the Department of the Environment's statutory Lists of Buildings of Special Architectural or Historic Interest (revised since the mid 1980s), available for consultation in local planning departments and some libraries.

General Works on Architecture:

On churches: *Cathedrals and Abbeys in England and Wales* (1979), and *Churches in the Landscape* (1989) both by Richard Morris; the latter also has useful background information on village building. John Summerson, *The Classical Language of Architecture* (1979) is an admirable introduction to its subject. General histories which can be recommended are N. Coldstream, *The Decorated Style*, 1994, John Summerson, *Architecture in Britain 1530–1830* (Pelican History of Art, latest ed. 1991); R. Dixon and S. Muthesius, *Victorian Architecture* (1978); A. Service, *Edwardian Architecture* (1977). M. Girouard, *Life in the English Country House* (1978), describes how houses were used through the centuries. H.M. Colvin, *A Biographical Dictionary of British Architects 1600–1840* (latest ed. 1995) is the essential reference book to architects and their works. S. Brand, *How Buildings Learn* (1994) discusses how buildings are altered and adapted.

Further reading on particular topics:

Landscape and Building Materials
K.J. Allison, *The East Riding of Yorkshire Landscape* (1976) is essential reading on the history and development of the landscape. The best general book on building materials is A. Clifton-Taylor, *The Pattern of English Building* (1972), with a detailed look at brickwork provided by R. Brunskill, *Brick Building in Britain* (1990). On local building materials there is F.W. Brooks' article on Hull's medieval brickyard in the J*ournal of the British Archaeological Association* (1939) and A. Lazenby, *The Cobble Stones of Holderness* (1994). S. Neave has written on the use of thatch in the East Riding in the *Yorkshire Journal* (1993) and D. Neave on 'Pantiles: Their early use and manufacture in the Humber Region' in D. Tyszka et al. (eds.), *Land, People and Landscapes* (1991).

Medieval Ruins
Good brief accounts of castles and monastic houses in P.F. Ryder, *Medieval Buildings of Yorkshire* (1982). More general coverage of castles in *Memorials of Old Yorkshire*, ed. T.M. Fallow (1909) and of earthworks and castles in *Victoria County History, Yorkshire vol. 2* (1912). B. English, Lords of Holderness (1979) provides background on the builders of Skipsea Castle and information in *The Northumberland Household Book* (1905 edition) brings early C16 Wressle and Leconfield 'castles' to life. Brief histories of all East Riding religious houses are given in *Victoria County History, Yorkshire vol. 3* (1912) and details of the foundation and early history of the major houses in J. Burton, *The Religious Orders in the East Riding of Yorkshire in the Twelfth Century* (1989). There is a full account of the late-C19 excavation of Watton Priory in the *Transactions of the East Riding Antiquarian Society*, vol. 8 (1900).

Medieval Church Design
J.E. Morris, *The East Riding of Yorkshire* (1906 and later editions) remains an invaluable guide to medieval churches, providing references to relevant journal articles. The most able accounts of individual churches are those by the architect John Bilson, including studies in *Archaeologia* of Beverley Minster chapter house (vol. 54, 1895), Weaverthorpe (vol. 72, 1922) and Wharram-le-Street (vol. 73, 1923) and in the *Yorkshire Archaeological Journal* of Newbald (vol. 21, 1911), Howden (vol. 22, 1913), Beverley Minster (vol. 24, 1917) and Beverley St Mary (vol. 25, 1920). C. Wilson (ed.), *Medieval Art and Architecture in the East Riding of Yorkshire* (1989) contains essays on the churches of Howden and Patrington, Bridlington Priory, and the early history of Beverley Minster. C. Wilson has written on 'The Early Thirteenth-Century Architecture of Beverley Minster: Cathedral Splendours and Cistercian Austerities' in P.R. Cross and S.D. Lloyd (eds.), *Thirteenth Century England III* (1991) and Ivan Hall on the Georgian restorations in Georgian Group Journal (1993). Of the popular guides to Beverley Minster the most useful is the well-illustrated Pitkin Guide (1990) with text by P. Rogerson. Beverley Minster is the subject of *The master builders – the construction of a great church* (1991), an English Heritage video.

Medieval Churches: Furnishings and Fittings
Early Christian monuments and carvings are exhaustively covered in J.T. Lang, *Corpus of Anglo-Saxon Stone Sculpture*, vol III: York and Eastern Yorkshire (1991). C. Wilson (ed.), *Medieval Art and Architecture in the East Riding of Yorkshire* (1989) has studies of East Riding sepulchral monuments before 1500, the Percy Tomb workshop, monumental brasses from the York workshops and the medieval stained glass and misericords of Beverley Minster. The many musical carvings in the Minster are examined by G. and J. Montagu in *Early Music* (July 1978). Other valuable studies of medieval monuments include S. Badham, *Brasses from the North East* (1979) and P.E. Routh, *Medieval Effigal Alabaster Tombs in Yorkshire* (1976). For East Riding fonts see E.M. Cole in *Transactions of the East Riding Antiquarian Society* vol. 10 (1903), and F. Mann, *Early Medieval Church Sculpture* (1985). P. Dirsztay, Church Furnishings: A NADFAS Guide (1978) and T. Cocke et al., *Recording a church: an illustrated glossary* (1982) are useful handbooks.

The Jacobean Great House
M. Imrie, *The Manor Houses of Burton Agnes and their Owners* (1993) is a well-researched history of the manor house and hall. Burton Constable has been the subject of numerous studies by Ivan Hall including *Burton Constable Hall* (1991) with E. Hall, and the most recent guide (1994). L. Ambler, *The Old Halls and Manor Houses of Yorkshire* (1913) includes accounts of Burton Agnes Hall and Burton Constable Hall. For background see M. Girouard, *Robert Smythson & the Elizabethan Country House* (1983) and M. Airs, *The Making of the English Country House 1580–1640* (1976). D. Hey, *Buildings of Britain 1550–1750: Yorkshire* (1981), provides regional coverage.

The Country House and its Setting
On Sledmere House and grounds there are articles by J. Popham in *Country Life* (16 and 23 January 1986) and an entertaining account of the rebuilding 1911–17 in B. English (ed.), *East Yorkshire Miscellany 1* (1992). Much has been written on the Sykes family including *The Visitors' Book* a well-illustrated work by C.S. Sykes (1978). Excellent background material on local landed families is provided by B. English, *The Great Landowners of East Yorkshire 1530–1910* (1990) and J.T. Ward's booklet on *East Yorkshire Landed Estates in the Nineteenth Century* (1967). For East Riding country houses there are numerous articles in *Country Life* and the *Transactions of the Georgian Society for East Yorkshire* and brief accounts in *York Georgian Society Annual Reports*. The setting of the country house is explored in D. Neave and D. Turnbull, *Landscaped Parks and Gardens of East Yorkshire* (1992).

County Town
The Victoria County History: East Riding vol. 6 (1989) provides the most detailed account of the history and institutions of Beverley. For an admirable short history see K.A. MacMahon, *Beverley* (1973). Earlier history and buildings are covered in K. Miller et al., *Beverley, an archaeological and architectural study*, Royal Commission on Historical Monuments (1982). The architecture of the town is thoroughly covered in I. and E. Hall, *Historic Beverley* (1973) with a useful survey in A. Clifton-Taylor, *Six More English Towns* (1981). B. Moody, Doorways into Beverley's Past (1991) concentrates on one particular architectural feature. For comparable urban buildings see the Royal Commission on Historical Monuments of England (RCHME) volumes on the *City of York*.

Victorian Churches and Chapels
R. Dixon and S. Muthesius, *Victorian Architecture* (1978) has a good introduction to Victorian church architecture. For the two most prominent architects see A. Quiney, *John Loughborough Pearson* (1979) and J. Hutchinson and P. Joyce, *George Edmund Street in East Yorkshire* (1981). See also J. Bayly, *Four Churches in the Deanery of Buckrose* (1894) and B.F.L. Clarke and J. Piper, 'Street's Yorkshire Churches and Contemporary Criticism' in J. Summerson (ed.), *Concerning Architecture* (1968). J. Allibone, *The Wallpaintings at Garton-on-the-Wolds* (1991) is a detailed and well-illustrated account of the sumptuous Victorian interior. Contemporary accounts of C19 restoration and rebuilding occur in local newspapers, the *Associated Architectural Societies Reports* and *The*

Ecclesiologist. D. Neave and S. Neave, *East Riding Chapels and Meeting Houses* (1990) provides an illustrated catalogue of Nonconformist buildings. A handful of the most prominent are covered in more detail in C. Stell, *Chapels and meeting-houses of Northern England* (1994). D. Neave, *Lost Churches and Chapels of Hull* (1991) records over 150 demolished, disused or converted buildings.

The Rural Scene 1750–1900
On agricultural history see A. Harris, *The Rural Landscape of the East Riding of Yorkshire* 1700–1850 (1961), K.J. Allison, *The East Riding of Yorkshire Landscape* (1976) and O. Wilkinson, *The Agricultural Revolution in the East Riding of Yorkshire* (1956). One particular type of farm building has been examined in C. Hayfield, 'Manure Factories? The post-enclosure high barns of the Yorkshire Wolds', *Landscape History* 13, 1991. For general background see R.W. Brunskill, *Traditional Farm Buildings of Britain* (1987) and S. Wade Martins, *Historic Farm Buildings* (1991). Some East Riding farmhouses and cottages are included in B. Harrison and B. Hutton, *Vernacular houses in North Yorkshire and Cleveland* (1984) and B. Hutton, 'Timber-framed Houses in the Vale of York', *Medieval Archaeology* (1973). Comparative material from adjoining area is in the RCHME volume on *Houses of the North York Moors* (1987). Useful material on local domestic architecture from the Middle Ages until the early C20 is included in S. Egerton, *Housing in Humberside* (1989). D. Neave, 'The Architecture and History of Houses' in B. Dyson (ed.), *A Guide to Local Studies in East Yorkshire* (1985) gives guidance on local sources. On industrial buildings there is a fair coverage of East Riding buildings in J. Hatcher, *The Industrial Architecture of Yorkshire* (1985) and there are detailed surveys of *East Riding Water-mills* by K.J. Allison (1970) and *East Yorkshire Windmills* by R. Gregory (1985). Blacksmiths' shops on the Yorkshire Wolds are dealt with by C. Hayfield in D. Tyszka et al (eds.), *Land, People and Landscapes* (1991). The East Yorkshire Local History Society has produced excellent short accounts of transport development, e.g. B.F. Duckham on inland waterways (1973) and K.A. MacMahon on turnpike roads (1964) and railways (1953), but little has been published on physical remains. K. Hoole *Railway Stations of the North East* (1985) has good material on local stations designed by G.T. Andrews.

Seaside Resorts
Resorts are covered by the relevant East Riding volumes of the *Victoria County History*: Bridlington and Filey (vol. 2, 1974), Withernsea (vol. 5, 1984), and Hornsea (vol. 7, forthcoming). See also D. Cookson, *Seaside Resorts in Humberside* (1987) with an emphasis on Withernsea, D. Neave, 'Transport and the Early Development of East Riding Resorts' in E.M. Sigsworth (ed.), *Ports and Resorts in the Regions* (1980) and M. Fearon, *Filey from fishing village to Edwardian resort* (1990).

The Port of Hull
The older histories of Hull by Hadley (1788), Tickell (1796), Frost (1827) and Sheahan (1864) have been superseded by the excellent *Victoria County History* volume (vol. 1, 1969) and E. Gillett and K.A. MacMahon's *History of Hull* (1980). J. Markham, *The Book of Hull* (1989) is a well-illustrated introduction. Brief accounts of the trade and shipping of the port from the Middle Ages to the C19 are given in the series of booklets published by the East Yorkshire Local History Society (nos. 17, 27, 31 and 43). The city's buildings from the C17 to early C19 are dealt with in I. and E. Hall, *Georgian Hull*, a lavishly illustrated and thoroughly researched account. M.E. Ingram, *The Maisters of Kingston upon Hull 1560–1840* (1983) has good material on the various houses of one merchant family: Maister House, Hull, White Hall, Winestead, and Wood Hall, Ellerby. The history, but not architecture, of the country houses of Hull merchants is fully charted in *'Hull Gent. Seeks Country Residence'* 1750–1850 by K.J. Allison (1981). Some of the demolished houses are illustrated in D. Neave and E. Waterson, *Lost Houses of East Yorkshire* (1988).

Architectural Styles in Hull 1830–1930
Victorian buildings are dealt with in two detailed, but dated, theses, on 'Architecture of the Victorian Era of Kingston upon Hull' by I. Goldthorpe, and 'Nonconformist Churches in the Hull District' by B.W. Blanchard (both Hull School of Architecture 1955) available in Hull Local History Library. An illustrated article on 'The Architecture of our Large Provincial Towns–XIV–Hull' in *The Builder* (2 April 1898) is a useful contemporary account. The two volumes of drawings of Hull by F.S. Smith published under the title of *Images of Victorian Hull*, by C. Aldridge (1989), and C. Ketchell (1990) have much information on C19 and earlier buildings. On Hull's best known Victorian architect see D. Linstrum, 'Cuthbert Brodrick', *Royal Society of Arts Journal*, January 1971. See also A. Stuart Gray, *Edwardian Architecture : A biographical dictionary* (1985) for early C20 architects.

Housing in Hull: Victorian to Modern
Hull's distinctive type of working-class housing is fully surveyed in C.A. Forster, *Court Housing in Kingston upon Hull* (1972); the middle class developments of Pearson Park and 'The Avenues' are examined by C. Ketchell (ed.), *An Illustrated History of the Avenues and Pearson Park, Hull* (1989). Dates given in J. Markham, *Streets of Hull: A History of their Names* (1987) provides clues for charting C19 development. Good illustrative material can be found in S. Egerton *Housing in Humberside* (1989). See also J. Low, 'The Founding of Hull Garden Village', *Landscape Design*, February 1983. B. C. Skern, *Housing in Kingston upon Hull Between the Wars* (1986) is a slim account of interwar council housing. The subject is more fully explored in A.M. Kerr, 'Variety in public sector housing: a study of architectural and social differentiation in selected council house areas of Hull' (unpublished M.Phil thesis, Hull University, 1979). For general background see J. Burnett, *A Social History of Housing 1815–1985* (1985), S. Muthesius, *The English Terraced House* (1982), and H. Barrett and T. Phillips, *Suburban Style: The British Home 1840–1960*. For other Yorkshire examples see L. Caffyn, *Workers' Housing in West Yorkshire 1750–1920* (1986).

Modern Architecture
Information on post-war architecture has to be sought in contemporary architectural journals and local newspapers. For background see V.M. Lampugnani (ed.), *Encyclopaedia of 20th-Century Architecture* (1988).

Other relevant English Heritage publications for teachers include in the **Education on Site** series:
Tim Copeland, *Geography and the historic environment*, (1993); Tim Copeland, *Using castles* (1992); Cynthia Cooksey, *Using abbeys* (1992); Richard Morris, *Churches, cathedrals and chapels* (1995); Gail Durbin, *Using historic houses* (1993); Crispin Keith, *Using listed buildings* (1991); Sallie Purkis, *Using school buildings* (1993); Sallie Purkis, *Using Memorials* (1995).

Acknowledgements:
We would like to thank the following for providing illustrations: James Austin, BM Photographic Services, British Steel, Susan Cunliffe-Lister, Durham University, Barbara English, Geoff Howard, J. Hugh Martin Partnership, Humberside Archaeology Unit, Humberside County Archive Service, A.F. Kersting, Christopher Ketchell, Margaret Imrie, Ivor Innes, Richard Morris, Dominic Powlesland, RCHME, RJB Mining (UK) Ltd, Eddie Ryle-Hodges, Sir Tatton Sykes, University of Hull. The maps are by Arthur Shelley and Reginald and Marjorie Piggott.

OPPOSITE PAGE: The Waggoners' Memorial, Sledmere.